I Hope you Enjoy! is ... (handwritten inscription)

END OF THE thin blue LINE

THE ANATOMY
of an
OFFICER

BASED ON ACTUAL EVENTS

WRITTEN BY

K. W. ALLEN

Contents of an Officer

A WORD from the AUTHOR

The perversion of authority:

"A corrupted monarchy shall assuredly breed organized anarchy. Just as failure to condemn such abhorrent behavior, shall assuredly condone such abhorrent behavior."

—K. W. ALLEN

Kristopher W. Allen

INTRO

In today's society in America, police and citizen encounters seem to have an unsettling commonality between them. The difference in equality and fairness with concern to the treatment between a person of color and the privilege of being white in America, is substantially prevalent. The thing about this is, this issue is not a new standardized problem nor is it an acceptable one. With the combination of a dogmatic style media coverage and an already engrained disdain for police officers in general, you would think that a major part of police academy training, is not to train at all.

When society is constantly force fed a strict and steady diet of enraging, targeted video of the vulgar actions from a small percentage of prejudicial, incompetent and biased police officers, hate and fear-mongering seem to take a priority.

There are thousands upon thousands of good officers that do good work in society and then there are the ones who allow perversion to take over their professional principles. Provoking societal outrage, the media will flood the airways with on scene reports and footage of officers making permanent life altering decisions in split seconds and then follow that story up with an uninformed and incomplete report about those same officers. Then, there's the "edited video syndrome," where they show viewers video of whatever popular narrative that's circulating social media at the time, regardless of the actual truth shown on the unedited version.

Failing to report a complete, accurate and impartially balanced story, the so called "fair media" neglect to mention the painstaking facts. Facts that make a world of difference to the average citizen. As a result, this practice breeds an unforgiving and finite portrayal of Police Officers vs. John Q. Citizen, ultimately betraying society.

See, the media has a tendency to put out information that is good for their ratings and what's good for themselves and only themselves. But that's their job. A job of, "suitable half-truths." When it comes to stories that deal with law enforcement and society, the media rarely broadcast good news. If no one they deem important gets hurt in the process, then it's not worth mentioning, at all. This brand of perpetual idealism pits citizens and officers against each other more than necessary or desired.

End of the Thin Blue Line, or ETBL, is the remedy for the constantly illusive facts sometimes associated with being a law enforcement officer. It's an informative analysis that provides transparency and enlightenment. Exciting and edifying, it ushers in a truth baring account of law enforcement, shining a bright light on some of the many different elemental aspects that an officer can encounter while enforcing the law.

Mastering the matrix of the mind, life and duty of a police officer is a challenge that very few people possess the capacity to navigate. In this first-hand account fostered by an eighteen year career in policing the streets of Detroit Michigan, I will attempt to guide you through the anatomical functions of law enforcement. Maintaining the integrity of case facts, certain names will be changed in order to preserve the assurance of anonymity.

Places like the City of Detroit and its' surrounding urban communities are exceedingly prime examples of what every part of the world aspires to emulate. Enriched with a multitude of different cultures, languages, religions, races, beliefs and socioeconomic class, Detroit is a metropolitan melting pot. Although plagued as a city familiar with being labeled with either placing somewhere in the top three, or even taking the number one spot for the F.B.I.'s most violent cities in America, policing citizens remain universal.

During this informative, exciting and intense trek through the eyes of a soul that forever bear the footprints of the brothers and sisters that answer the call in blue, we will touch on case work that is considerably sensitive, horrific and at times miraculous and heroic. This provocative insight on policing society is an uncensored look at not just the many types of crime and the ways they may play out, but it will also show the dramatic divergence between you working the job and the job working you. Officers are often exposed to the most traumatizing and horrific parts of humanity...both psychological as well as physical.

ETBL allows you to witness how the often frustrating situations can produce that balance between positive and bitter outcomes. End of the Thin Blue Line also shines light on that infamous dark secret that's kept so obsessively close to the vest by most officers who become its victim. Victims of a shameless and possessive psychiatric cancer...PTSD. Formally referred to as "shell shock," Post Traumatic Stress Disorder is a fairly new label, but remains a difficult diagnosis to control. With the characteristics of a trained assassin, PTSD can prove to be a formidable enemy, designed to destroy. With this in-depth and very personal glimpse into the life altering events of an average officer's career, this diversified biography will open the door to acknowledging the signs and triggers of this life threatening ailment.

End of the Thin Blue Line is a much needed fresh dose of reality that illustrates how the job can both, be the best reward in life, or silently take its toll on the lives of both, officers and citizens, alike. Most law enforcement officers have a calling to the job that reach back all the way as far as childhood. Some are generational; others experience things as a child that dictates that career choice; though it might be something with even more subtlety to it. Something like, a favorite television show, or maybe that pair of plastic handcuffs with a cap gun and badge.

Whatever the source; whether it be crime, tragedy, or life itself, there will forever remain the necessity for someone, somewhere to help society maintain a functional civilization. Being in law enforcement is a calling that must be answered but not just by anyone. Solving a strangers life-long problems within ten to fifteen minutes takes a special kind of person. A person that has the ability to compartmentalize without compromise.

Kristopher W. Allen

CHAPTER / one

Policing America

From the beginning of the first minute of the first shift on the job as an agent of the law, until the conclusion of their career, law enforcement officers wield a prodigious measure of power and authority. Sometimes a lesson in history along with a refresher on the basics can help to sustain a professional objective, guiding that officer towards a more gratifying career in policing America.

Championing the nickname "Cops," a term used in Britain since the 1700's, born of the Latin word "Capere via," meaning to grab, apprehend or capture. Then again from its adopted American moniker, "Coppers," said to have originated from the coppered star badges that officers wore. Police officers are the most relevant and existential entity for societal order. Cities like New York, Philadelphia, Boston and Chicago were among the first few cities to adopt the concept in the 1800's. By the late 1880's, all major cities in the U.S. had established a sustainable police force.

With the beneficial element of preventing any and all unforeseen future acts of criminal activity, policing has always been a reactive enterprise. Originally referred to as constables, the practice of law enforcement officers have been in existence since at least ninth century Rome.

A young country at best, America remains stagnant in its adolescent stage. After the Revolutionary and Civil wars, we still find ourselves at war. A war of equality.

Every human being is blessed with the ability of preference. The curse of preference is the inability to control the prejudice that preferences breed. Unchecked, a persons' prejudices can cause apocalyptic consequences.

Monarchies, dictators and oppressors are some of the surnames given to a single person and or persons of power that possess the ability to mistake prejudicial incompetence for progressive leadership. From world wars to bullying, misguided and perverted prejudices possess the ability to counter act its own intention, destroying everything in its path.

Racism may be one of the oldest forms of bullying, but it is a bastardized derivative of power. Power can dilute the nature of man. The profound effect goes back to the beginning of time itself. An eye opening concept of morality, born of authors before its' final conjurer, and is best coined by The Baron, John Emerich Edward Dalberg Acton, in a letter to Bishop Mandell Creighton in 1887 reads the prophetic phrase of, "*Power tends to corrupt, and absolute power corrupts absolutely.*" This idealistic and proven statement is a crowning measurement of ones' own being. It shines a blinding light on the historical tendencies, that as a person's power increases, their sense of morality diminishes.

Buried under mounds of time and struggle, America as we know it, hasn't changed much since its conception. Ill-conceived and misguided, its' core fiber is forever stained with the blood of its' native settlers, whom still remain victims. But the atrocity didn't stop there. See, their new land needed structure. A structure that was built on the backs of another horrific concept; slavery. Malice and the use of force is its first nature. Foreign settlers entered the new world and decided that the way of the land should be ruled similar to how their former European land was ruled. So they implemented their laws, their rules, and their regulations into their new world.

Adopted over more than a hundred years before a centralized municipal police department first emerged in the United States, the use of a police force was used as a slave patrol to detain, question and punish slaves discovered traveling without papers...and not necessarily in that order. Their responsibilities varied from place to place according to the needs of the community. Such as Carolina's slave patrol in 1704, which were exclusively hired to chase slaves.

Realizing that the theft of this corrupted idealism could not withstand the challenges of the new world, they knew that something revolutionary was needed in its place. So after several failed attempts, a revolution is what they accomplished. In 1787, the founding fathers and other delegates gathered in Philadelphia in an attempt to come up with some type of functional government for this new world.

In order for the new world to grow into a united America, a Constitution was conceived by a syndicate totaling fifty-five men, but only ratified by thirty-nine. Now, officially adopted in 1788 as the law of the land for nine of the original thirteen states, the continental congress announced that this new form of government would actually take its' first breath in March of 1789. With this birth of America's new federal guide to governing, its authoritative footing was firmly structured around three separate branches of government; executive, legislative and judicial. By all appearances, they intended to establish and promote fair government with fundamental laws that guaranteed basic rights for all of its citizens. But it was only the beginning. Just two years later, they added what is now known as the First Amendment, guaranteeing the freedom of speech and religion. From its' primordial ten amendments to its current twenty-seven, the original Constitution's concepts remain archaic and unfinished. Leaving America with a divide that literally fractures its own people into multiple permutations.

This is where we are today in society as a whole. Divided by beliefs, politics, misconceptions, personal prejudice, racism, sexism, classism, on and on and on; law enforcement must remain resolute to such grievous afflictions.

Policing America, falls in the realm of the judicial branch. It is the frontline to serving and protecting the country's population. It has also, historically been a tool used for the abuse of that certain classification of citizen, and has become even more taboo than ever. With the world watching, America and its practices are at center stage. Unlike, just twenty-five to thirty years ago, cameras are virtually everywhere you turn, and someone is always watching. The easy access to social media is so profound, that even a toddler can use it. This fact does not bring difficulty to policing. Instead it brings accountability to a profession that professes to protect and serve.

"Tyrannical power and riches of the flesh are not enough payment to fix the CORRUPTION of the spirit. Therefore, the soul SHALL pay." -- *K. W. ALLEN*

These words of wisdom apply to more than just the perverted monarchies and the disillusioned wealthy who foolishly sacrifice their moral posture for a temporary societal advantage and or monetary positioning. Whether it be a simple cooperation, reward or a place of peace in life, treating others with respect have unexpected benefits and yet, remain a lost art.

As the laws of man are made up of morals that are relatively based on religious principles, so are the ramifications. For example, to apologize and ask for forgiveness is one of the simplest commonality between the two. Both are acceptable, yet still remain liable to its own set of consequences. It is the combination of morality, respect, duty and honor of the individual officer that help to distinguish the good from the bad.

Character is a category that cannot be ignored nor covered up. America and its people have a goal of beginning new times, but are constantly bogged down by its history. Still ingrained in an ethnic divide, citizens of America remain torn. The ignorance of history is not an excuse, but an enabling crutch that allows us to make the same mistakes over and over, without progress; passing the burdens on to our children, clearly blinding societies' bright future.

Serving as a police officer will bring many challenges. Personally and professionally, an officer will commonly be torn by the two. It is at this point that that officer use his or her own good judgment. Knowledge and experience are the foundation of a successful encounter...but, principles, morality, the rule of law and regulations are an important balancing act also. These are the tools needed to help shape and guide every officer in becoming a better, more effective professional in law enforcement.

Police academy training teaches student police officers the rule of law and regulations as cornerstone guidelines. With a turn around that usually lasts no less than six months, young cadets endure several categories of intense training. Educated in the art of procedural and hand to hand combat tactics, government, state and local laws, departmental regulations, precision driving, cultural diversity and much more, a level of professionalism is the final product. Obligation and commitment is assumed when the oath that every officer takes upon the successful completion of the academy, is pledged. It is at that moment that he or she is charged to blindly enforce the law without prejudice or favor. Once graduated, officers gain the authority and legal obligation to essentially supervise society.

The concept of ordering, directing or commanding an individual or individuals can present a challenge. Even so, with someone who possesses a decent level of actual legal intellect. It can, by itself, hinder an officer's ability to effectively complete his or her duties. This is a common cause of conflict.

Over the course of a police officer's career, that officer will unwittingly on occasion, come in contact with a seemingly every day civilian who thinks that they may know more about the law than the police officer does. Although rare, that little detail can admittedly be factually accurate. Yet, at the time of the encounter between the two, the police officer shall retain the authority until instructed otherwise by a governing agent of law enforcement. Because the officer is acting in an official capacity, the civilian may not revel in that fact of superior knowledge and begin to resist. At that precise moment, the officer should think. Never react to a persons' demeanor, personally. The officer must use established rule of law, their training and, think. Take a moment to consider options. Is this person attempting to provoke a response? Could this person be distracting me from something else? Is this person mentally challenged? It could be a plethora of things and that officer must sift through all of it, quickly. The situation can evolve into an uncontrollable matter within seconds. The trick is to have a set of goals while policing. One, should always be the safety of yourself and your partner. Second, should be the safety of the person or persons you're dealing with. Personal morals and principles can play a big part in a successful resolution. Third comes the law. Although enforcing the law will be the ultimate goal, it can, at times, become a second, and even a third option.

Even though every officers' personal primary goal isn't necessarily to enforce the law, but to first and foremost make sure that they make it back home to their own families, you will read, sometimes, that primary goal takes a back seat to what needs to be done.

Kristopher W. Allen

CHAPTER / two

Baptized in a Murderous Inferno

The life of a police officer can often be, rewarding; but more than often, it's unforgiving. Filled with ups, downs, success and failures, you ultimately hope that by the end of your twenty plus year shift, you would've repaired or saved more lives than you may have impaired or destroyed in the pursuit of law enforcement.

With this extraordinary and intimate look into the mind of a police officer, you will discover several things along the way. Mainly about how being a police officer does not exempt you from being a human being. And unfortunately, human beings come with faults like prejudices, preferences and an affinity for life; including self-preservation.

In the police academy, you're taught a multitude of standards like federal, state, and local laws, regulations, procedures and trade skill. -But that is the extent of it. Having the privilege of becoming a police officer means applying every bit of life that you've ever experienced inside and to a great degree, outside of the academy. Experiences like emotion, technique, physicality, beliefs, principles, morals, skill and most importantly, patience; the capacity to tolerate or except. This tool is a mental weapon that can grant you mind over matter when it comes to observation and investigation.

After some time as an officer who learns and build on the experiences of real life circumstances, both professional as well as personal, you acquire the subtle things that make policing effective and safe. Those finite cues will become a permanent part of that officer for the rest of their lives. He or she will unknowingly apply that skill to virtually every decision they make; socially, domestically, financially, even religiously.

Although being a police officer is classified as just a job, it can creep into your every day and become your very life. It can wake up with you, vacation with you and even go on that big first date with you. Selfishly, it can take over your entire existence without you even knowing it. In most cases, it can be a good thing. You develop a heightened sense of awareness of your surroundings. How people carry themselves, the bulges on their body, the fact that there is no obvious useful reason that that person is standing there, appearing to linger. You'll be off duty with your family, dining at a restaurant, visiting a bank, even attending service in church and at times, you'll find yourself uncontrollably profiling people. You'll begin detailing that certain persons' facial markers, memorizing license plates, playing out that "just-in-case," scenario in your mind and going as far as to analyze as much of your current environment as humanly possible.

This type of mental calisthenics can keep the brain sharp as well as yourself and others, such as your family, safe. But there's a negative in this constant methodical mental exercise. It can cause an unnoticed origin of stress in your life. Unchecked, that cancerous stress can slither its' way into your relationships with the important people in your life, such as your significant other or your children. It can even show up at your workplace, where you deal with hundreds of different people with thousands of personalities each day. People that come with issues and an unforgiven propensity for conflict.

Generally, a person wants to become a police officer to make a difference. To change that person or person's life, positively. But in the process of making such a masterful stroke of influence on a stranger's life, you'll find yourself having to break a few eggs to bake that cake. An officer always starts off with certain personal goals. Help the children of the inner city, stop the criminals in the neighborhood where that officer grew up and parents still live in. Join SWAT to look cool. Maybe even take a shot at easing a family's pain while working in homicide, otherwise known as, "the murder police." Although these are just some of the many internal departmental divisions within a police department, all of the divisional departments are paved with good intentions.

But being the police means owning that unshakable second shadow. That shadow that is rarely talked about. Masterfully avoided and hardly ever confronted, that relentlessly cunning, second shadow can meticulously drain your soul like sand passing through the bottled neck of an hour glass. If you're not careful, taking a loss can take away your peace and force you down a dimly lit path. But here's the kicker; taking a win, can take a different, but just as equally important type of piece from you too. A piece of your friends, family, your faith and sooner or later, a piece of you. The job is not meant for everyone...it's meant for that certain one.

-CASE HISTORY-

It was fifteen minutes before the end of Officers Grant and Mathews' shift...the curtain call to a long and hard day. The end of a humid August week, Friday's shift finally submitted to another promising mid-summer's weekend that lay in wait like a wild cat ready to pounce. Excitement peaked to weekend prospects, fueled by the idea of the ungodly heated day finally laboring its way towards a much needed and well deserved end.

Officer Mathews pulled into the police employee parking lot to unload the day's foraged provisions and begin the scout shut-down process. Both Officers, with a mindset of elated calm, started up a battle of banter. As Mathews carefully explained to Officer Grant the reason why his mother wears a gun belt on Wednesdays and Thursdays and no belt on Fridays and Saturday, a run is dispatched.

"Four-Ten. Scout, Four-Ten...make One-Two-Nine, Clark and assist Fire." Dispatch read off.

Working Four-Ten, Officer Brown along with Officer Simmons responded... "Show scout Four-Ten on the way radio."

Looking forward to getting off work on time and getting that well-earned weekend started, Officers Grant and Mathews continued their daily duty dismount, but kept a close ear to the radio just in-case something popped up.

Four-Ten called in, "Four-Ten at scene, Radio."

Dispatch responded, "Four-Ten. Four-Ten, I have you at scene."

The run board was clear and Four-Ten's run was literally across the street from the police station where Grant and Mathews were prepping for off duty. Thinking that Four-Ten would only be busy assisting the fire department with its usual traffic issue, Mathews and Grant head towards the precinct doors with arms full of equipment and paperwork to finish up. -Then...

"FOUR-TEN, EMERGENCY PRIORITY, RADIO!" Brown shouted with a tone of panic to boot. "We've got an active shooter on scene, inside, Radio. Repeat, there is a person with a weapon inside."

Without hesitation, or taking another breath, Brown notified Dispatch and whomever else that was listening on that channel at that moment.

"We're going in.", he exclaimed.

Knowing exactly where Four-Ten was located, Mathews and Grant wasted no time. They literally dropped everything they had in their hands right where they stood.

"Four-Two in route to back. Thirty seconds out." Mathews said calmly over the air, even though his body was currently dumping loads of adrenaline into his system.

Then, other scouts called in to dispatch and rushed to the call for help as fast and safely as they could.

"Four-One, heading over there."

"Four-Seven, on the way."

"Four-Nine, coming from the deep, south."

Without haste, all available precinct patrolman scrambled towards the unknown peril. Time was an enemy from all sides now.

As Four-Two pulled up to the location, they called at scene. "Four-Two at scene, Radio."

The chaos was heavily present and obviously trying its best to take control of the scene. Officer Grant and Mathews skidded to a halt, quickly jumped out of the scout car and, for a split second...reality. Somewhat entranced, they immediately surveyed the ensuing anarchy...

Thick, heavy smoke bellowed high into the air, smothering the top two floors. Out of control flames shot out of just about every top floor window. It was obvious that the fire started on the top fourth floor, but it was almost impossible to get to. Firefighters frantically scrambled to set up the hoses and ladders.

Frenzied and seemingly frustrated, the Firemen shouted, "We need you!"

Hanging and swinging from the third and fourth floors, desperate victims were screaming for help as they made the choice of jumping from broken out windows to escape the rabid, murderous inferno.

Suddenly, one shot rang out followed by four more shots. It was apparent that this four story apartment building was burning from inside out, but it was equally apparent that there was a gun battle going on inside, and Officers Grant and Mathews knew they had to get in there, fast.

"Shots fired Radio!" Mathews informed dispatch.

Without thought of that, revered self-preservation, Officer Mathews and Grant sprinted into the densely smoked filled building. They had to, lives were at stake. Then, just as they got inside of the front door, a flurry of gun shots rattled off. They could feel the bullets passing in the air all around them. They scurried for cover.

"Four-Ten Radio! We're taking fire! We need back up now!" they shouted.

"Four-Two is there, Four-Ten." Dispatch relayed in an attempt to reassure Four-Ten. "Where are you at?" Dispatch asked.

No response...

Gunfire constantly rang out as Officers Grant and Mathews entered the building. But the old buildings' walls and structure caused the sounds to echo and bounce aimlessly around. Time was preciously running out and there was a stairwell that led up, towards the obvious danger, and another that led down into the unknown. In that split second of entering this highly probable death trap situation, Officers Grant and Mathews decided to do something that no partners should ever do...they split up.

"Which way?" Mathews asked, in a hurried state.

Officer Grant pointed up the stairs, "Go that way," he shouted. "I'll check down there."
Still unable to see no more than about fifteen to twenty feet in front of them, along with not having a clue of the layout to the building, Mathews chose to take the raised first level as Officer Grant took the lower level.

"Police Officer coming in!" They both repeatedly yelled out as they entered the building, as not to be shot or shot at by friendly fire.

With his gun drawn, Officer Grant cautiously walked down the smoky stairwell that led into the murky clouded hallway. Steadily moving forward, into a deathly fatal funnel, Officer Grant knew he must move smartly. Remaining wary and alert, Grant used every bit of sense God gave him.

Still no response from Four-Ten, with the intensity building he moved closer and closer. He couldn't hear anything coming from under the stairs. The distinct aroma of gunfire became stronger as he meticulously advanced.

"Grant! Here we are! Down here!" Four-Ten yelled out as he reached the bottom of the stairwell. Apparently, their radios wouldn't allow them to transmit a response to anyone, because of the material of the aged building's walls.

Like a mother giving birth to their young, the two officers, still with guns drawn, emerged from that long hallway filled with the thick cloud of smoke and gunpowder as if it were straight out of a movie, but this was all happening live and in living color.

"I found them, Radio. Lower Level. Let my partner know." Grant advised Dispatch. "Where's the shooter?" Officer Grant eagerly asked as he stopped in his tracks.

Still, with guns drawn, they both eerily pointed over Officer Grant's shoulder.

Knowing he had just checked where they were pointing to, he still turned and aimed in. But it was a storage area, located under the stairs. With no light, it was just too thick with the smoky fog. The visibility was impossible.

Officer Grant raised his flashlight, and bravely moved in. Though the floor, coated with a brass tone, was riddled with spent shell casings, the thick and hazy, white veil was much thinner towards the ground.

He cleverly scanned the area along the floor for the gunman's feet, nothing. Knowing that the threat had to be neutralized, Officer Grant left his cover and moved in closer.

"You better come out, or else I'mma have to start shooting. And I don't miss," Grant warned.

Still, nothing.

Please man. Don't make me have to kill nobody today," Officer Grant continued his warnings in an attempt to get whomever it was, that was armed and hiding to realize that the reality of accepting the idea of defeat was his best chance in living to see another day.

Still, nothing.

By now, all three Officers are cautiously scanning the area, but don't observe any movement anywhere.

The crew of Four-Two stood ready behind Officer Grant as he crept two steps closer. In another fatal funnel, he realized, there's nobody hiding in front of them.

"I don't see anything, do you?" Officer Grant asked Four-Two.

They both concurred with a "No."

As Officer Grant backed out he looked at all the spent rounds on the ground, now paying attention to everything else that wasn't a perp with a gun. The damage the rounds took to everything. The marble stairs, the railing, the wall. Then he saw it. The wall... It had two holes.

Grant quickly pushed the two officers back and kicks at the deep and hollowed bullet hole in the wall over and over. The first kick caused no sound or movement, so he continued to force the hole to open wider with repeated strikes. After about four or five kicks, the hole was large enough to shine a flashlight inside for a peak. Officer Simmons of Four-Two kneeled down to shine his light and gun muzzle inside and there he was... The lifeless body lay there in a thick puddle of his own blood.

With a twisted feeling of satisfaction, the threat was over and everyone felt a lot safer.

"Perp is down, Radio. Send an EMS and a supervisor to our location." Brown eagerly advised.

Officer Simmons retrieved the gun as Officer Brown took a strong grip of the perpetrators' ankles, and plucked him from his dark hiding place. That's when they saw it...the large exit wound through the back of his head.

Turned out, the gunman had just recently shot and stabbed three people inside of one of the fourth floor apartments...and then set it on fire. Realizing that the police had him trapped, with no way out and taking fire, he took his handgun, placed it inside of his own mouth, and willfully pulled the trigger...ending his enraged killing spree.

Meanwhile, Officer Mathews, Four-seven, Four -one and Four-nine were busy kicking in door after door, going from apartment to apartment, evacuating the entire building, escorting and assisting the fire department, which included one of the gunman's victims that survived the assault and the fire. He later claimed that the perp caused all of that carnage because someone owed him twenty dollars.

-CONCLUSION-

Common sense and experience beg to offer an alternate, possibly more sinister reasoning for this evil person's actions. Whatever the case may be, this is but one of many examples of what police officers are charged with and are willing to do for each other but more importantly, for a stranger. Some people are born with that will and drive...some aren't. Having countlessly witnessed officers not make it to the end of shift the way they began, or heartbreakingly, not at all, coupled with the knowledge and experiences of a seasoned officer, and yet still put your own life, as well as your family and friends' peace, in peril, requires a fortitude that is both illusive as well as immeasurable.

CHAPTER / three

Dad's Closet

Equipped with the knowledge of law, regulations, and a good amount of common sense, along with every kind of street smarts learned from your environment growing up, as an officer, you don't avoid the danger, you run to it. Policing the community that you have grown fond of, you tend to press forward as if it were your own family in danger.

-CASE HISTORY-

Officers Quinn and Mills were driving along, having a typical day on patrol working Scout Four-One. Answering calls to that same, everyday house alarm, the abandoned car left in the backyard of a vacant home, intoxicated male causing a disturbance or simply stopping by their favorite gas station to grab a quick snack. Halfway in the day, everything has a normal sense to it. So their blood pressure's leveled out and then they get that call. That call that every officer dreads.

"Scout Four-One. Four-One. We're getting Shots Fired.One down." Dispatch read off.

Now, the attention of both officers sharpened. Their heart beats picked up. Their body was now naturally dumping enough adrenaline to make an actual sane person see double. But they can't. It's time to focus.

Dispatch gave them the address. "Make one-two-three-four Scotten," then follows up with the details. "Father came home and found his seven year old son unresponsive and bleeding from the head."

By now, every officer tuned in to the channel has stopped what they were doing in order to rush to help Four-One with this unspeakable tragedy.

Immediately and without thought, Officer Mills' right foot instinctively pressed down on that gas pedal a little bit harder.

"Let's get there, but let's get there in one piece." His partner reminded him. "We gotta get there," he encouraged.

Dispatch then warned them, "The father found his handgun lying next to his son on the fathers' bedroom closet floor."

Officer Mills gradually developed tunnel vision. Now, relying mainly on instinct and his partners' skill to help get themselves to that destination with no delays and in one piece, his stress level rose with his heart rate, as the correlation between this possible fatally injured child and his own child of similar age began to creep into his mind. An equation that will ultimately affect every decision that they both will make with this case from that point on.

Riddled with adrenaline, a sense of urgency and compassion, Officer Mills and Officer Quinn force themselves to stay focused with rational thinking, procedure and training. Basically, they are ultimately attempting to turn their humanity sign off in order to hit the professional auto pilot. This is not to say that this process is a good or a bad thing...but it's definitely a necessary thing.

Lights and sirens... Right, left. Left, right. Cutting through traffic like a hot butter knife, Officer Mills drove like the professional he was.

Officer Quinn pointed at the house as they approach. "There it is!" he exclaimed.

"Four-One at scene, Radio! E.T.A. on EMS?" Quinn inquired.

"Ten minutes out, Four-One...ten minutes." Dispatch responded.

They came to a stop and jumped out of the scout car with such focus. Getting into that house was the only thing on those officers' minds at that time. Everything they had going on before that moment, didn't matter. Baby mama drama, bills, that person that cut them off on the way to work that morning, nothing. It was personal.

Knowing that there is a handgun definitely in the house, they still take precautions. They drew their weapons from their holsters. They also know, no knock is required. Exigent circumstances apply in this situation.

They pushed their way through the door...

An in shock female is just sitting on the living room couch. She looks up, but is frozen and can't speak.

"Where's the boy?" Officer Mills yelled.
His voice echoed throughout the home. "Where is the boy at?" he repeated with an ever-dwindling patience.

She finally pointed to a back bedroom, just to the right of the officers.

As if they had blinders on, Officer Quinn physically shoved the huge family pit bull to the side as Officer Mills flipped furniture out of his path as they scrambled to get to their young victim.

What they walked into, they still can't even talk about without a quiver in their throats to this day.

The father on the floor uncontrollably sobbing, holding two crimson red bath towels that used to be white. Kneeling over his son, he shouted, "Wake up Son. Brian please wake up!"

"Four-One, Radio. That's a confirmed shooting." We need EMS, now!" Quinn told Dispatch as clear and plain as he could at the time.

Meanwhile, Officer Mills retrieved the handgun, grabbed the father, and politely told him, "Move!"

Time is a funny thing when you don't have any.

"No time Mills," Quinn calmly told his partner.

He bent down, and with his finger, he pushed the young boys brain matter back into the hole in his head, wrapped it up with one of those bloody towels, picked the boy up and sprinted back to his scout car, leaving the grieving father behind.

"You stay here, Sir." Officer Quinn explained to the father. "Someone will be here to come get you."

"Radio! Show us in route to the hospital with that seven year old boy." Mills informed Dispatch.

"Okay. What route are you taking?" Dispatch asked.

Mills gave out his route as he was driving. "South on Scotten to Chrysler and then north to Children's Hospital," he replied. We need somebody to lock down that scene for us, Radio." he continued.

Four-Two quickly chimed in and volunteered. "Four-Two will take that, Radio. We're pulling up now."

"Okay, Four-Two. I have you holding the scene there for Four-One." Dispatch responded.

The urgency of the moment was so powerful that by now, Scout Four-One was half the way to the hospital as that transmission transpired.

Blood streamed down from the boys head as he lay cradled in Quinn's arms, he spoke to him. With a calm that only a veteran officer can muster, he told him, "It's okay. Your name is Brian, right? Okay Brian, we're gonna go to the doctor and get you all better, okay?"

"How's he lookin' Q?", Mills asked with a heavy heart.

"He's okay. You're okay, aren't you B? Yeah. You're a tough one." Quinn replied with the prospect of hope and optimism.

Drenched in blood, Officer Quinn held on to the hope that they were making a difference by not waiting that extra time for the EMS. Another split decision first responders have to sometimes make.

They pulled up to the hospital as the medical staff were out there eagerly waiting.

"Has he opened his eyes or said anything?" The nurses and doctors asked.

"No..." Quinn replied with dread.

They placed him on a gurney and franticly wheeled him inside. Now, the wait.

As they sat and awaited the result of all the hard work that the medical staff was putting in, that inevitable foe returned...reality.

The nature and rawness of what just occurred starts to breed shock for both Quinn and Mills. But is this normal for an officer? Do they need to speak to someone? Or is this something you're supposed to work through on your own?

After about thirty minutes, the doctor exited the O.R. and broke the news to the officers. Staggered, they continued on with their duty.

They returned to the boys home where the father anxiously remained, detained and awaiting the news of his son.

Officer Mills and Officer Quinn knew that there had to be a strategy to do what they had to do. It was imperative to break the news to the father, but keep him as under control as much as possible, because his day wasn't going to get any better any time soon.

With mixed emotions, they explained to the boy's father that the doctors did everything they could, but his son just never woke up. Then they placed him under arrest for neglect.

Later, the father was also charged with a felon in possession of a firearm, violation of parole, the five pounds of marijuana hidden behind the hundred stolen boxes of shoes that his son used to climb up, giving him access to the handgun that sadly ended his life.

-CONCLUSION-

So many things will occur to you as a police officer and other first responders from the time you first get the emergency call to service to the time you actually arrive, that if you stopped to think about it, it would be too late.

The challenge is while keeping in mind that you have to get there fast, you have to get there. That means avoiding any and all delays. Traffic, construction, accidents and or scathingly relentless weather. Emotions can intensify with any police run where the similarity hits home.

Though duty is first, the goal is to save lives by any means. That means rules and regulations might not always apply to every given situation. An officer must use good moral judgment, safely. Failure to understand the difference within such moments can prove to become a reckless and unrecoverable mistake.

CHAPTER / four

You Can Run, But...

The three religious responsibilities of a police officer are to save lives, enforce the law and keep the peace. Sometimes these ideals and principles go hand and hand. Not always in the same order, but they are definitely the textbook definition of what an officers' duty demands.

In the process of upholding and enforcing the law, some citizens get caught up in the gears of that monstrous machine, and get crushed. And unless the officer bares some sort of unhealthy prejudice towards that citizen or situation, and for some unknown and unacceptable reason, cannot remain fair, objective and professional, it's neither foreseen nor intentional of what may transpire during or after an encounter.

-CASE HISTORY-

At the beginning of the power shift, Officers Jones and Smith attended roll call to receive their assignments. During that roll call, Lieutenant Benton issued a challenge, a reward type contest.

"It's cold out," he said. "Now, I don't want anyone going out there and killing themselves trying to get this done..."

The Lieutenant took a slight pause in his announcement... Unable to keep a straight face, he cracked open a slight grin.

"It's bad out there, and visibility sucks, ice under the snow, and they said the temp is supposed to drop. So, today we're gonna play a little "Slide Game." Slide time to the crew who puts in a little work," he suggested.

Now, the "Slide Game" ritual that some shift supervisors use, are sometimes used to accomplish several goals. The challenge rules are simple. The typical challenge usually would require something such as, the scout with the most citations half way through the shift, or the first scout to make a weapon or a drug arrest, wins. The reward is that, that first scout to accomplish the goal, would get to slide out and go home early. This management tactic bread competition and drove up shift stats.

Being fairly new to the job, Jones and Smith still retained that closed-minded academy training, youthful eagerness, and an unpolished technique.

With just a couple of years on the job each, Officers Smith and Jones received their assignments, retrieved their equipment and quickly set-out to get that, "Go home early golden ticket." They were working on regular patrol as scout Four-Eleven, but is any patrol, regular?

In typical partner banter, Officer Jones took the first jab of the day, "Yo, Smitty we bouta go do this, man. Right off the ramp. I left the iron on at the crib and your lazy-ass girlfriend won't get up out the bed to turn it off."

Officer Smith smiled and with a quick and witty retort, he replied, "Yeah, she does that. That's why I prefer your mother most of the time. At least she got enough sense to turn the iron off when she's done pressin' my draws."

As if Chris Tucker said it himself, Jones replied with, "Don't be talkin' about my mamma, man!"

This is the way most partners that ride around for eight to sixteen hours a day, every day, communicate. It's a survival instinct. No one wants to be on edge, depressed or bored to death every day. So they crack jokes on each other, and talk about home life and current issues of society, often. They become closer than most of their own family members.

After their short, back and forth mockery, they loaded up and headed out.

"Where should we head to first, Jones?" Officer Smith asked.

"You know what spot we're bouta go to." Jones replied.

"Holden?" Smith queried.

"Hell yeah...you know how they do up there." Jones responded.

"Cool. Let's go, then... I want her to do another load before I send her back over to you." Smith continued to dig in with his trash talk.

Now, the area of Holden wasn't a large residential area, but it was known for its high volume of narcotics that blanketed the carved out twenty block section of the precinct. Another, little well known fact is, Holden was riddled with a plethora of people who made it a religious sport to drive around, dirty.

"Driving dirty," is an endearing urban term that references the moment a person with warrants, no vehicle paperwork, carrying drugs or possibly an illegal handgun, hop into the driver's seat of a car and drive around, unlawfully.

As they slip and slide through the Holden street neighborhood, the weather became even worse by the minute. And with bad weather, usually came the typical computer connection issues. They either run slow or freeze up all together.

Not long into the shift, they observe something out of the ordinary. A brand new vehicle pulling away from a known narcotic location. But what was so abnormal about it was that, the driver looked about fifteen years old, at the most, with the drivers' side window wide open in the middle of a winter storm.

Maybe he momentarily lowered it. Fresh air, heat flashes, ate a bad taco. Or just maybe, it could be broken out and the vehicle was actually, stolen. At this juncture, it wasn't clear. But prior criminal experience suggested that it was a high probability that a crime had just reared its ugly face, creating the situation of a fact based suspicious abnormality.

"You see that?" Officer Smith asked Jones.

"Yep... You see he avoided eye contact?" Jones responded.

"Yep," he replied.

They quickly catch up to the vehicle, punch the license plate into the computer and wait for his mistake. Two seconds later, traffic violation.

Officer Smith activated the lights and then hit the siren switch, twice. "Chirp, chirp."

Surprisingly, the vehicle pulls to the side immediately. They notify dispatch of their location as well as a description of the vehicle as they pull up behind him.

With the weather becoming increasingly worse with every second that passed, they couldn't wait for the computer to come back up.

They exited their scout car, and reluctantly entered into the freezing January weather. The snow was so thick and heavy, visibility was down to only about half of a block.

Officer Smith exited on the passenger side and walked up to the questionable vehicle. "Watch him," he warned Jones.

Jones stepped out on the drivers' side, "I got'em," he replied.

Hands on their, still, holstered weapons, Officers Jones and Smith approached the questionable vehicle with a textbook academy technique.

Jones cautiously walked up to the missing driver side window.

"Yes sir?" the young man says with his hands clearly raised in the air showing that he wasn't holding any weapons.

In an attempt to calm and defuse confrontation, deescalate the situations or give the illusion that the officers could relate to the person that they were potentially about to arrest, Officer Jones gave the appearance of familiarity with a simple universally familiar question...

"What's up?" Jones asked.

"Nothing," he answered. "I'm just on my way from my girl's house. She's pregnant," he replied.

Skepticism steadily builds.

It's a well-known fact that whenever someone voluntarily gives up way too much and unnecessary information, they're usually attempting to distract. Especially when it's super personal.

"Okay. Can I see your driver's license, registration and proof of insurance?" Jones asked.

With Officer Smith on the suspicious vehicles' passenger side, watching everything going on inside the vehicle, the driver shouldn't stand a chance of getting the jump on either of them, if he was armed, right?

"Can I reach in my back pocket to get it?" the young man nervously asked.

Knowing their surroundings and being familiar with the average crimes that consistently plague the area, both officers remained ready.

"Sure," Jones responded.

"May I ask what I did, Sir?" the driver inquired.

"Sure. You didn't use your signal when you made those two lane changes back there," he explained.

Officer Jones then noticed that this young man is extremely nervous. But not the regular, "Oh damn...I'm about to get this ticket" nervous. It was an unsettling, "I'm hiding something," anxious type of nervousness.

Frantically he began frisking himself, checking every pocket he had trying to find his information.

"I noticed your window there. Is something wrong with it?" Jones asked. "Aren't you even a little cold?"

He handed Officer Jones his license, but no paperwork. Suspicions instantly rose even higher.

"Oh. It's broken," the young driver claimed with a smile on his face.

"Broken, or broken out?" Jones questioned.

The driver nervously smiled even harder. Aww naw, nothing like that. It's just broken," he explained.

"Oh, okay. So, you don't have any of the paperwork?" Jones asked as he took a quick peek at the license, noticing the young looking teen was actually eighteen years old.

Kristopher W. Allen

"Do I have any of the paperwork? Umm, I must've left it in my other pants pocket," he said.

Now every cop in America knows, that as soon as a person responds to a question by repeating the exact question asked, they're trying to come up with a lie, quickly.

Officer Jones lets out a chuckle, "Hmm, hmm."

Jones now knows for a fact, that the driver is full of it. In an attempt to keep the extremely nervously young man calm, Officer Jones told the driver, "Ok, that's cool. Don't worry about it. But I'mma have to write you that ticket for the lane violation, okay? It's bad out here and we don't want anyone to get hurt."

"Yessir...I understand," the young man replied.

Without knowing if the computer was able to retrieve any information or not, they tell the driver to put his keys on the roof of his vehicle and to stay put, while they go get the information that they needed from their computer for the ticket. Another deescalation tactic to make him think that he's only getting a citation while at the same time disarming his means of a possible getaway.

56 | P a g e

Officer Jones slowly backed back up to the scout car as his freezing partner followed his lead. They got back into their car and then made one of the most important decisions they'd made all day. They cranked the heat up to tropical levels.

"Man! It's freezing out there," Smith exclaimed.

"I think I saw Jesus," Jones joked.

"There was glass all over the floor. What did he say?" Smith asked.

"He's dirty," he summed up with his reply.

As they warmed up, began writing the ticket and awaited for the ever unreliable computer, they kept at least one pair of eyes on the nervously suspicious driver. Finally, the computer popped on and started spitting out all kinds of information.

"Look," Smith said. "It's stolen."

For a split second, they both looked down at the screen, but at the same time in that split second, the driver hopped out of the vehicle and ran.

Jones looked up. "Oh shit! He's running," he shouted.

Without hesitation, they both leapt out of their scout car as Officer Smith yelled into his mic. "Radio Emergency! Priority!"

He quickly transmitted the description of the fleeing felon. Direction, race, gender, age, height, weight and clothing.

"He's running south bound from our location wearing a blue and orange striped skull cap, orange coat vest, blue jeans, and brown Timberlands," Smith advised.

But five steps in, they simultaneously realized, they couldn't see him anymore. Just like that, the snowy white-out had swallowed him whole.

"Damnit!" Smith exclaimed with frustration.

"He's gone," Jones intelligently pointed out.

Discouraged, Officer Smith notified Dispatch, "Disregard Radio. We lost'em."

Left with only to recover the stolen vehicle, they knew that more than likely, their "Golden Ticket" wasn't gonna happen that night.

"I guess we're here all night, partner." Smith said with a sarcastic smile as they returned to their scout car.

Jones grinned as he shut his door.

"What are you smiling about? Ya boy just took a poof pill," Smith commented with a slight amount of agitation.

"He ran like your girl left his iron on too," Jones cracked.

Smith couldn't help but laugh, "Whatever, man. Let's call this in and get a tow," Smith suggested.

"Alright. You call it in and I'll go inventory the inside right quick," Jones added.

Now, this stolen vehicle is not a small vehicle. In fact, it's a very large Ford Excursion. So Jones knew he was probably gonna be out in the elements a little longer than what he had desired, while his partner sat snuggled inside the cozy comforts of the scout car, but the large truck had to be cleared of all and any possible weapons, currency, and illegal property, such as a hundred unopened iPhone boxes, or maybe even three-hundred thousand dollars, worth of cocaine.

"Holy Shit!"

He opened the back doors and every item that was just mentioned, poured out onto the snowy covered concrete.

"Smitty!" he shouted. "Look at this shit."

Smith exited his warmed nest and drug his astonished fallen jaw through the snow.

"The fuck?" he exclaimed in disbelief. Eyes bulged, he looks at his partner,"Did you put that there?" he asked jokingly.

"Call for another car and a supervisor," Jones suggested.

What they'd just realized were the extremely dangerous factors that now plagued their situation. See, they were dead smack in the middle of a very dangerous area. Visibility was horrible and back up would have a hell of a time cutting through that thick snow.

Smith and Jones were out there all by themselves, with a large amount of product with a huge street value and with that amount in jeopardy, they knew that one scout car crew wouldn't discourage the owner one bit.

Coupled with the fact that they had no idea where the driver fled to and, or if, he would return, they placed the things that spilled out onto the streets back into the truck and returned back to their cruiser.

"He could've went to strap up and get deep with who knows how many people. He could be back at any time, Smitty," Officer Jones reminded his partner with concern in his voice.

"I know," Smith replied. "Just keep your eyes open."

As they sat, anxiously awaiting for back-up, the snow, thankfully, began to let up. Visibility became crystal clear.

"Definitely here for the night Smitty," Jones told his partner.

"Yeah, but your moms though," Smith continued with the witty jousting.

"Shut up!" Jones said, smiling ear to ear as they begin laughing again.

After a few more pin and needle minutes passed, the back-up crew, supervisor and tow truck finally arrived.

The driver never returned and the illegal items that were bursting out of the paraphernalia filled truck as well as the truck, itself, were meticulously cataloged and placed on evidence.

Unable to slide out and go home early, Four-Eleven resumed their function and continued patrolling for the remainder of their shift.

With only three hours remaining in the shift, scout Four-Eleven received a call to service from dispatch.

"Scout Four-Eleven...Four-Eleven. Make Pinewood and Michigan. The fire department had a needs police to make the scene. They say they found something that requires P.D. to make the location," Dispatch read off.

"Four-Eleven in route," they responded.

"What do think this is all about?" Jones asked.

Tired and ready to go home, Smith answered his partner, "I don't know. I'm just glad we already ate, because there's no telling what's waiting up in there."

As they pulled up to the house, they could see that it's completely torched and wondered, what could be so important that the fire department needed the police department so eagerly.

"Here we go," Jones reluctantly expressed as they stepped out of their warm and comfy scout car.

A fire captain walked up to Four-Eleven and said, "I'm glad you guys got here so fast."

Officer Jones shook his hand and inquired, "What's up Captain?"

"Follow me," the captain said as they all carefully walked into the soot filled home. "My guys were putting out this massive fire, and when they worked their way into the basement, where it appears to have started, they discovered something."

Brewing over with anticipation, Officers Jones and Smith couldn't figure out why no one could just tell them what it was that they were supposed to be doing there.

Still smoldering, they made their way down to the basement level.

"Okay Captain, what's the issue? What's the big secret?"

"I told your dispatcher. They didn't tell you?" the Captain asked.

"No... They just told us to meet and assist you guys with something you found," Officer Jones replied.

The captain pointed to another room and said, "He's over there."

"He?" Who is he?" Smith asked with total confusion.

Officer Jones walked into the room. "Shit!" he exclaimed.

"What?" Officer Smith asked as he turned the corner and walks in. "Awe, shit..."

Hard to tell for sure at first glance, because of the damage done by the fire and whomever was responsible, they moved in closer in order to confirm what they thought they were looking at.

Both, in disbelief, looked on at the results of an unforeseen and awful consequence of simply being an officer and doing the job.

Tied to a chair, still wearing his orange coat vest, blue jeans and brown Timberland boots, sat the decapitated, chard remains of the young eighteen year old that fled earlier that night, leaving that lethal street amount of product that spewed out of the rear end of that truck to be confiscated and placed on evidence by police.

After further investigation, it appeared that the violently deceased young man was known to be a car thief from another neighborhood. Apparently, the vehicle was sitting in a driveway, parked and warming up, when he decided to break-out the driver's side window and steal it. But he stole the wrong ride.

Someone observed scout Four-Eleven impounding the Ford truck and informed the owner of the contents inside, that his product was in police custody. The owner immediately put a hit out on the young car thief before Four-Eleven was even done processing the evidence.

At just eighteen years of age, this young man made a decision that brought an end to his own adolescent life, and changed the lives of both Officer Smith and Jones...forever.

-CONCLUSION-

Accepting the duty of becoming a police officer, carries a wide range of responsibilities. Responsibilities that are prepared for, as well as the unpredictable ones that are unimaginable and impossible to prepare for. Officers enter the lives of random citizens daily. Though the purpose is to ultimately bring peace and justice into their situation, the process can be ugly at times.

Professions such as doctors, nurses, counselors or coroners, peace officers try very hard not to take what they experience in the performance of their duties, personal. To be able to master the ability to compartmentalize certain tragedies is a struggle that stands on the shoulders of every man and woman to dawn a badge. But sometimes, it's seemingly impossible to not walk around with those stones of affliction that weigh you down, daily.

Kristopher W. Allen

CHAPTER / five

PSALMS 23

"Yea, though I walk through the valley of the shadow of death, I will fear no evil: for thou art with me; thy rod and thy staff, they comfort me. Thou preparest a table before me in the presence of mine enemies: thou anointest my head with oil; my cup runneth over. Surely goodness and mercy shall follow me all the days of my life: and I will dwell in the house of the Lord forever." – Psalms 23

This is a scripture that pinpoints an emphatic and poignant presence of mind that every officer experiences. Religious or not, the commonality of death, loudly knocking at the door is an inevitability.

Cities that operate with such a wide range of various social and economic capacities, command a unique embodiment of characteristics that breathe life into a super metroplex of social and cultural diversity.

If you're fortunate enough to be born and raised in the hustle and bustle workings of an inner city with such characteristics, cities like Los Angeles, Detroit, Brooklyn or Chicago, you pick-up a few things along the way.

Things like behavioral tendencies, the introduction and lesson plan on how to instantly detect when you're being hustled or deceived. How to relate and ultimately communicate with an array of different cultures, genders and ideology practices. More importantly, you enroll in a lifelong subscription on learning how to keep your guard up, avoiding situations that subscribe to unhealthy encounters. Encounters that occur often in an officer's career and command a high probability of plaguing your family with tears of agony that intrude in the dawn of loss.

-CASE HISTORY-

As if it had just transpired twenty minutes ago, Officer Love recalled his story with the clarity of a flawless diamond. With a series of somber toned quivers in his voice, Officer Love gave it everything he had as he steadied himself before he dug deep within his emotional scarring in order to narrate his life altering saga. With a slight hesitation, Officer Love returned to that horrible day. The day that the devil decided to rear his ugly head out of the ground with the unholiest of intentions. So unholy, you dare not blink first.

It was a frigid and cold December afternoon. Just fifteen days away from the years' most annually celebrated family holiday, when life decided to issue a friendly reminder of how precious it can be.

After a fun late night out on the town, the morning started off like any other day.

As usual, his villainous alarm clock yelps out a horrible noise. That, wake up! It's time to go to work, sound. It seemed to be more of a sacrilege tone to his ear, than any kind of modulation of reverence at the time.

Although, a Stevie Wonder song was set to play for his alarm, all he could hear in his mind was an obnoxious, buzz.

Startled, Officer Love jumped up, awaking from his comatose state. "What the hell?" he mumbled to himself in a mist of confusion.

With an unforgiving hangover, he glanced at the clock and realized that he missed his first two wake up alarms.

"Dammit!" he exclaimed in frustration.

He quickly gathered himself together, grabbed a bite and hustled his way out the door.

On his way in to work, he realized that he was partnered up with one of his closest friends, Officer Fitzgerald. So he figured that he'd have a pretty smooth day. What he didn't realize is that no day in the life of an officer is predictable. Smooth is wishful thinking at best.

Officer Love went into the locker room to retrieve his gear and to let his partner know that he was there and that they were going to have a great day.

"Fitz, what-up? You ready to get out there?" Love asked.

"Man, they must've been extremely high on life when they made that schedule. They really went and messed up this time. They put you and me together? It's on, partner!" Fitz replied.

"Hell yeah!"

They both geared up and headed to roll call to receive their assignments.

"Attention to roll call," Sergeant Adams chimed aloud and then announced, "Fitzgerald, Love. You guys will be working, scout Two-One."

Sergeant Adams continued his roll call; giving all twelve of his officers their assignments. He informed them of the days on going issues and departmental updates. As he dismissed everyone, he concluded with a reminder for everyone to watch each other's back and to make sure that they all made it back to off duty roll call.

Officers Love and Fitz stocked their vehicle with everything that they needed for their tour and headed out.

"Fitz, I had a long night last night, man. We're gonna really take it extra easy today Bro," Love strongly suggested.

"No problem with me, kid. I was up all last night with my new born anyway."

"How is he doing, by the way?" Love asked.

"He still has a little fever. We're watching him closely though," Fitz responded.

"Man, I hope he's ok," Love replied with concern.

"Thanks, man. I hope so too," Fitz acknowledged.
"Now let's go get something to eat. That little piece of dry toast didn't do anything but make me mad," Officer Love suggested. "Plus I wanna ask you something."

"You can ask me now, Partner," he replied.

As they pull into the parking lot of their favorite restaurant, Love put the car in park, looked over to Fitz, and with a straight and extremely serious look on his face, Love asked, "Little fella is not starting to look like me, is he?"

Fitz begins cracking up. "You're stupid, man," he responded.

"No? Not yet? Not even a little?" Love continued with his antics.

"Shut up, clown!" Fitz replied, still laughing.

They were greeted by a bright smiling waitress who guided them to a table and they ordered their food. Love was always good for a joke or two to get the morning started off right.

As the shift progressed, they received pretty simple police runs. Recovery of a stolen vehicle, road hazard, school crossing, even an assist a stranded motorist call.

Time was passing fairly smoothly until six hours into their tour, Fitz received a call from his wife. She explained to him that their son wasn't getting any better and that she was going to take him to the doctor's office.

Worried, Officer Fitzgerald decided that because the day was running so smoothly and almost done, that he would just request to leave early to check on his ill son.

"He's still the same," he explained to Love. "That over the counter stuff that they suggested is not working. She wants to take him in and see what the doctor says."

"Cool. Call Sergeant Adams and let him know you have to head out early. I'll get you back to the station in no time," Love offered.

They pulled up to the station minutes later, "Keep me posted on the little guy's progress," Love told Fitz.

"Of course, I'll hit you up later and let you know," he responded as he got into his personal vehicle.

"Don't forget," Love shouted.

"I won't. I won't," Fitz reassured him.

Love smiled and told Fitz, "I just wanna know if he has my nose or what."

Fitz grinned and let out a well needed laugh. "Shut up, dummy. I'll hit you up."

Fitzgerald pulled off and Officer Love returned back in service as a now, one-man Adam unit. "Radio... Show Two-One as a one man unit for the remainder of the day," Love informed Dispatch.

"Two-One-Adam. I have you back in service as a one man unit," Dispatch responded.

Officer Love returned back to patrolling and assisting other units for the remainder of his tour. As the day wound down, scout Two-Three received a police run.

"Two-Three. Two-Three. Make 4459 East Stabler Street. That's 4459 East Stabler Street on a disturbance. Possible person with weapon. Caller says that their neighbor is threatening to shoot people on the block. No weapon seen at this time," Dispatch relayed.

Knowing that the shift was coming to an end, they hurriedly responded, "Two-Three in route, Radio," with the hopes that the run would be something simple and that it could be handled quickly.

Not busy on anything, Officer Love answered up to the call to assist. "Radio. Show Two-One-Adam making that location to assist that unit."

"Alright, Two-One-Adam. Two-Three, you have Two One -Adam backing you," Dispatch responded.

But while both units were on the way there, something else transpired. Something that would prove to be the beginnings of a soul searching journey that changed the course of life for everyone involved.

"Two-Three and Two-One-Adam, we're getting an update. That subject was just seen leaving out of your run location, waving around a hammer with blood on his clothes. Caller says they heard a woman screaming inside and now, it's completely quiet," Dispatch relayed to the responding units.

Picking up the pace, both units responded...

"Two-Three good on info."

"Two-One-Adam good on info also, Radio."

Hearing the run become even more dangerous, another unit decided to join the call, just in case.

"K-Nine-Seven-Four, Radio. Show me also making that location. I'm about five minutes out," he notified dispatch.

"Okay, K-Nine-Seven-Four. I show all three units in route," Dispatch replied.

Two-Three pulled up to the location and quickly exited their scout car. Noticing several droplets of blood leading in and out of the opened front door, they decided to enter under the exigent circumstances imbedded within the nature of the run.

They notified dispatch, "Two-Three at scene, Radio. We have an open door and no one is responding. Show us going in."

"I have you at scene, Two-Three. Use caution. Two-One-Adam and K-Nine-Seven-Four, Two-Three has an open door. Step it up!" Dispatch requested with their response.

Walking into the unknown, the pace of their heartbeats began to elevate. Their senses sharpened as they drew their weapons.

"Police!" they shouted. "Is anyone home?"

No one answered...

Searching the home, they carefully check each room, one by one as they continued to follow the blood trail that led into the house. It flowed in a deliberate path throughout the house like crimson red paint had discharged from the bottom of its damaged container.

As Two-Three continued to check the home, Four-Two-Adam and K-Nine-Seven-Four arrived to the location simultaneously.

Love notified dispatch first, "Radio. Show Two One-Adam at scene."

Then, K-Nine-Seven-Four, "K-Nine-Seven-Four is with him, Radio."

"I have you both at scene. Let me know what's going on when you get a chance." Dispatch responded.

"Copy that, Radio. Show us going inside," Officer Love replied as he and K-Nine-Seven-Four drew their weapons and cautiously entered the front door of the home.

"Police officers coming in!" they both shouted.

Just as Officer Love and K-Nine-Seven-Four entered the house, Two-Three radioed in, "Two-Three, Radio."

"Go ahead, Two-Three," Dispatch responded.

Dejected, they let Dispatch know that the perpetrator had already fled the location, and then somberly requested, "We're gonna need a supervisor and an ambulance for a confirmation at our location."

"Copy that, Two-Three. I'm notifying them now," Dispatch replied.

"You can have them go through the kitchen and meet us in the basement," Two-Three added.

"Copy that, Two-Three," Dispatch responded.

Knowing what that meant, both Officer Love and K-Nine-Seven-Four re-holstered their weapons and joined them in the basement.

Careful not to step in any blood evidence and contaminate the scene, they slowly walked down the squeaky stairwell, down into a dimly lit room. They turned as they reached the bottom step.

"Over here," Two-Three shouted out.

Love and K-Nine-Seven-Four shined their flashlight toward the crew of Two-Three. They took five more steps, and could see the bare feet of someone laying deathly still on the ground.

"Oh shit!" Love exclaimed in complete disbelief and disgust as K-Nine-Seven-Four staggered backward.

Madness and evil touched every part of that dark and moldy sub-leveled room. The walls were covered in such an ungodly amount of blood splatter. The smell of discharged feces and the mutilated remains of what turned out to be, the wife of the perpetrator.

They had a difficult time identifying the victim due to the damage that was done to her. It took a verification from the daughter in order to identify the deceased victim. She had just returned home as the officers had already been there for a while. Although distraught and unable to enter the basement, she was able to confirm a unique tattoo located on the shoulder of the deceased. The perpetrator used some kind of huge blunt object to pound and demolish her face, fragmenting every bone in her skull.

After a search of the interior, there was nothing to be found inside of the home that could even come close to achieving such a massive amount of damage. Especially the hammer that was last said to be wielded by the perpetrator.

At this point, all of the officers on scene had to place their emotions to the side and focus in on doing what they were trained to do, enforce the law.

K-Nine-Seven-Four gathered himself and returned back to his vehicle to retrieve his tracking K-nine partner. Determined to find the mad man responsible for such an abominable act, he unleashed his trained four-legged hunter to search the entire area. Having difficulty following the perpetrators scent because of the cold fresh snow, K-Nine-Seven-Four decided to grid search starting from the surrounding property.

Meanwhile, Officer Love contacted dispatch. "Radio, Two-One-Adam."

"Two-One-Adam, go," Dispatch responded.

"Yeah. Can you tell me where this call came from?" he asked.

"Yes. It came from just up the street at, 4465 East Stabler Street," Dispatch responded.

"Thank you, Radio," Love replied. "Show me making that location to get some additional information."

"Okay, Two-One-Adam. I'll show you busy making that location," Dispatch acknowledged.

As Officer Love headed up the street with the hopes of retrieving more intel on the situation, Two-Three remained inside, idling in that gruesome arena as they made all of their notifications.

Officer Love eventually located the 911 caller.

"Hello. You called 911, right?" he asked.

"Yes. I called," the caller replied.

"Can you tell me what happened or just what you saw?" Love inquired.

"Yes, I'll tell you everything that happened."

The caller explained to Love that the perpetrator was someone that they were having problems with earlier in the day. They continued on, saying that the subject was upset that they bought the home that he was illegally living in, from the county. They then added that the subject became even more irate at the demand that he and his family vacate the property, immediately. They said that, it was at that moment that the subject lost it, and began running around the neighborhood shouting and threatening to shoot anyone who came near his house.

Meanwhile, K-Nine-Seven-Four's grid search took him into the garage, located in the rear of the run location. That's where he found the murder weapon, in plain sight. Leaning in one of the dark cold corners of the garage, was the blood soaked tool used to commit the unimaginably heinous crime. It was a hammer after all, a ten pound sledge hammer.

K-Nine-Seven-Four notified dispatch to let scout Two-Three know that their "suspected" murder weapon was located in the rear of the run location, inside of the garage.

Two-Three acknowledged and then transmitted what was to become the most pertinent and life altering information in this case. "Two-Three good on that info, Radio. Tell K-Nine-Seven-Four thank you. Also Radio, we have some new information on our perp."

"Okay. Go ahead with your info, Two-Three," Dispatch responded.

"Yeah Radio, we have a name and a possible location on where this guy may be at right now," Two-Three said.

Dispatch replied, "Go ahead with your information, Two-Three."

Not knowing what was to shortly take place next, Two-Three relayed their information, "Okay, Radio. We're gonna be looking for a Victor Forte. He's a white male, forty-eight years old. Stocky build. About six foot two, two-hundred and sixty pounds. Bald, with a long dark colored beard. Last seen wearing a dark green coat, white shirt and blue jeans. The daughter told us that he was in an accident a few years ago and suffered a bad head injury. She said that he's not mentally stable. She also advised us that he sticks to a strict routine and is employed at a cleaners about five minutes from here. She suggested that he might be there."

"Copy that, Two-Three. Two-Three is he possibly still armed?" Dispatch asked.

"It's unknown at this time, Radio. The daughter doesn't know if her father owns any weapons, but anyone checking out that location should use caution," Two-Three replied.

"Copy that, Two-Three," Dispatch responded and then went on to repeat the description and possible location of the mentally ill assassin to all of the monitoring units.

Familiar with the cleaners that was suggested where the subject could have currently been, as well as the citizens of that particular area, Officer Love and K-Nine-Seven-Four immediately volunteer to go and check the location for the fleeing subject.

"Radio. Two-One-Adam. Show myself and K-Nine-Seven-Four making that cleaners location. We have a pretty good idea of which one it may be. We'll get you an address when we get there," Love advised.

"Two-One-Adam and K-Nine-Seven-Four, I show you both in route from your current location. Let me know when you pull up," Dispatch responded.

Without delay, they both answered, "Copy that, Radio. Will do."

Possessing experience, training and a lot of common sense, Officer Love quickly realized the level of potential chaos that could easily transpire in an instant. Especially when it relates to a person afflicted with a mental illness.

Both, Love and K-Nine-Seven-Four discretely pulled into the rear parking lot of the cleaners.

Officer Love notified dispatch that he and the other unit has arrived. Then he proceeded to relay to dispatch the address along with the name of the business.

"Thank you Two-One-Adam and K-Nine-Seven-Four. I have you both at scene," Dispatch replied.

As they exited their vehicles, they realize that the parking lot was full. Which meant that the inside was more than likely also full. Full of innocent bystanders.

With a hope that the mad man that had just committed such a horrific crime only moments ago was not inside, they strategically entered through the rear of the location. Thinking that if the subject was inside, he would never suspect that the police would enter through a rear employee door.

Armed with the clarity of situational awareness and two fully loaded forty caliber handguns, they opened the door and were greeted by a dark, poorly lit hallway with curtains on either side. Cloth draping hung heavy, lining their pathway. Nerves began to kick in as they cautiously walked inside.

They were startled when the eerie quiet was interrupted by a little boy running by screaming! He was being chased by his older sister. Both officers grabbed a hold of their holstered weapons out of reflex. Realizing that it was only two kids playing, they let out a healthy sigh of relief.

As they continued forward down what would soon become their valley of the shadow of death, they notice the lobby in front of them was full of women, children and elderly bystanders. It was a worst case scenario situation at best, if he turned out to be there.

With K-Nine-Seven-Four bringing up the rear, Officer Love took a few more steps forward and then one of the curtains flung open and a man walked out. Filled with shock and anxiety, Love jumped back a step.

"The hell?" he mumbled to himself. It wasn't Forte. It was only an employee. Once again, Love lets out a sigh of relief...

But just as he exhaled, a six foot two, two hundred and sixty pound bearded, bald white man, wearing a dark green coat and blue jeans, aggressively walked out right behind the employee.

Because Love took that step backwards when he was startled, and after emerging second from that draped off room, Forte had no clue that Love, nor his partner, were standing only a few feet away from his murderous intentions.

Before Officer Love could say anything, Forte reached into his coat pocket and pulled out a silver forty-five caliber handgun, and pointed at the back of the oblivious employees head.

Recognizing the depth of his situation, Officer Love knew he had to make a move, now.

"GUN!" Love yelled.

He quickly grabbed Forte's gun and knew he was in a fight for his own life.

Love's partner squeezed his mic transmitter button. "K-Nine-Seven-Four, Radio! He's here and armed. Send backup!" he exclaimed with panic.

Knowing that the place was packed full of families, Officer Love pulled the gun tightly to his own chest. Aiming the barrel directly into his vest as to minimize any carnage this monster intended, but he didn't fire.

The mortal tussle for life worked its way into the lobby as patrons began to scream and scatter; desperately scrambling to gather their loved ones and get to safety.

Unable to force the gun from Forte's monstrous mitts, he and Forte pulled and yanked back and forth, as Forte continued to fight for the weapon. K-Nine-Seven-Four saw the struggle for the handgun, drew his own weapon, but couldn't get a clear target. Love and Forte were just too close.

The strength of this beast of a man was beginning to tire Love out. Then Forte head butted Love dead in the nose. Dazed, Love continued to hold on for dear life. That's when K-Nine-Seven-Four grabbed Forte by the waist and tried desperately to get him to the ground. But he was already a large man and the power of a mentally ill person can grant them the strength of a super-powered human.

Unwilling to go to the ground, Forte released his weapon and turned his attention to K-Nine-Seven-Four. Love immediately tossed the weapon across the room and rejoined the fight. He hopped onto the back of Forte, wrapped his arms around his neck and attempted to choke him unconscious. But Forte was just too strong. The deranged monster somehow was able to quickly shake both Love and K-Nine-Seven-Four off, tossing both officers to the ground.

Fatigue was becoming a huge factor for both officers now. As the fight progressed, the population of patrons shrank to zero.

As both officers stood to their feet, Forte produced a second weapon; another hand gun.

Forte quickly determined his target. Time obviously decided to take a break at that point, because just as soon as he raised his weapon to fire, everything seemed to slow down to a snail's pace.

Forte aimed in on Officer Love.

With his partner thrown clear from possible friendly fire and realizing that he may be on his way into the greener pastures, Love drew his weapon as he stood to his feet.

As loud as a canon that had just been fired, a tiny, crystal clear snapping sound rang out, click..."

Forte pulled the trigger, but again, this gun didn't fire either.

Officer Love immediately aimed in tightly and fired until the threat was no more. Victor Forte was struck five times in his chest and throat. The damage from the bullets striking his heart and spinal cord caused him to die instantly.

Because of Forte's haste fleeing from his home, he neglected to load the first weapon that Love pulled tightly to his own chest to prevent any stray bullets from striking any innocent bystanders. The second weapon, miraculously misfired.

His malicious intentions to continue his killing spree by taking the lives of every employee and patron inside was prevented by two heroic officers who instinctively knew what was commandingly paramount.

-CONCLUSION-

This was a prime example of knowing the situation, the environment and the mentalities of all the people involved. An officer must understand that once they take the oath to serve and protect, there will be moments that the primary goal to preserve their own life first, can jump to a secondary option in an instant. Especially when innocent lives lay in the balance.

Kristopher W. Allen

CHAPTER / six

A Rookie Mistake

Most, that are raised in an environment that is of the opposite of what they police and those that were never exposed to life's lessons or its hardships, are at a disadvantage. Conflict resolution can be a new entity for them. Their experiences are not of the average person, so policing the average person can prove to be difficult.

Environments are a crucial factor in law enforcement. Not just the environments officers come across while executing their duties, but the seasoning environments that are procured through the personal exposure of life, in its entirety. Experience in a multi-cultural environment can be beneficial to effective policing. Exposure to the seventy percent of society that are considered to be of middle class is extremely beneficial. Because of the high percentage, a commonality is forged. This commonality fashions an ability to relate, understand and communicate effectively.

Officers possessing personal affluently sourced skills, can also be harnessed. Although, due to the smaller thirty percent left over, the commonality of upper class society is rarely utilized and can be lost in translation. This type of ingrained exposure will, undoubtedly, experience a longer, harder, learning curve. More than often they tend to overreact and actually become the cause of situations that range from an unnecessary harsh talking to, to an avoidable physical confrontation that could lead to a minor, possibly even fatal, injury. So, for an officer that is fortunate to be raised in a multicultural environment, you take advantage of the edge in which you were unknowingly blessed with. Blessed, because, you survived. Now you possess a healthy aptitude that can help someone else survive.

- C A S E H I S T O R Y -

It was 9:30 in the morning. A perfect summer Saturday morning. Birds are chirping, skies were blue, and the police radio was silent. People were still asleep from the night before, or just getting home from the night before. So far, everything appeared to be pointing to an easy going day. This is the misconception that many officers have. It's proof that they are only human. The mixture of hoping your day will be easy, or that you'll get off on time today, or maybe you'll even get that chance to take care of that thing you've been too busy to take care of all week. These are examples of nothing, but fuzzy distractions and empty hope. A police officer's day can go from zero to one thousand in a heartbeat.

Working scout Four-One-Adam, a single manned unit, Officer Tucker was patrolling his designated part of the precinct, when he overheard Officers Mathews and Cooper, both with only a year or two on the job, and working scout Four-Seven together get a police run to investigate a person causing a disturbance.

"Four-Seven, Four-Seven. Make Tillman and 23rd Street. We're getting several calls on a person loitering at that location. They say he's been drinking and playing loud music on that corner all night," Dispatch advised.

A description was given out of what the person to investigate looked like. Tucker, a veteran officer, had police runs to that area before. He had actionable knowledge of the everyday misguided endeavors that routinely emerge from the natural beast that is born of the streets. Endeavors that coincidently resemble things like, armed felons that frequent the area, a twenty-four hour street pharmacy and a history of recovered vehicles that remarkably, have no valid identification numbers that match anything on record.

He also had knowledge of, the "Jenkins." A family well known to other veteran officers that that particular family possessed a preferred proclivity for violent confrontations. This family had all the markings of an abridged mafia that just so happened to occupy several homes along that specific stretch of street. A street that is considered to be an area strategically classified as a, "Delta" area.

A designated "Delta" area is usually a small section of a city that is branded, highly dangerous. It's a tool created as a result of analyzed statistical recordings of multiple encounters and past criminal activity in that portion of the city. It's then highlighted to be a high risk, high crime sector. This classification is an alert notice that basically tells every officer patrolling and/or monitoring that area, to be on an even higher alert than usual. It's also a red flag for other unoccupied officers to assist any police unit that receives a dispatched run to that area.

"Show Four-Seven in route Radio," Cooper answered.

"Dispatch, show Scout Four-One-Adam making that location also, on the assist," Tucker apprised. "Also, be advised Radio, that area is a Delta area," he added.

"That's an affirmative Four-One-Adam. Four-Seven and Four-One-Adam, I have you both in route at nine-thirty-two, use caution," Dispatch advised.

Now, knowing what could happen at this higher than usual high risk location, the officers making the police run go through an experience very few people can deal with, especially multiple times in a day. Their bodies go through a type of transformation that can physically take a toll on, not only their own body, but it can affect the people around them also. It begins in the mind. The brain produces chemicals and signals that take control of the entire body. Like sexual seduction, confrontation demands the human body to react. Adrenalin begins to dump into the body. Anxiety kicks in which can cause the personality to change, demonstrating signs of irritability, poor concentration, even overreaction. Consequentially, both, adrenaline and anxiety, are the main ingredients to a physiological reaction, motivating the blood pressure to rise, sending more blood to the muscles and away from the organs.

These examples of physical and psychological reactions are processes that can be a recipe for productive results such as, that much needed state of a heightened awareness, but as it can be productive, it can also become, just as equally, unproductive. This normal human response can be a masterful composer for anything ranging from an avoidable weapons discharge, to simply just making a bad decision if you're not careful.

Scout Four-Seven made their way towards the run location. With their guard up, they approached the area with a peaked level of caution.

Riding in the passenger seat as the "Jump-Man", Cooper released the button on his holstered his weapon and slid it securely under his thigh, and rolled down his window so that he could hear his surroundings better.

"Here we go," Cooper remarked with a healthy build of excitement.

Mathews took his weapon out and placed it readily on his lap. "I'm ready," Officer Mathews expressed with a sense of comfort as he too, lowered his window.

Officer Cooper updated Dispatch. "Radio, show Four-Seven pulling up."

Four-Seven, I have you pulling up at scene at 9:41," Dispatch responded.

Both Officers, working scout Four-Seven, immediately survey the general area, keeping an eye out for anything or anyone that didn't quite fit the scenery of a peaceful sunny morning. Almost instantly, they spotted the described subject standing in front of a house located at the corner of Twenty-Third and Tillman.

The subject looked up as he saw the cruiser approaching and took a swig from a bottle in a brown bag.

"That looks like that might be him over there," Cooper pointed out to Mathews.

Blaring music still poured out from the interior of the car, he intimately leaned against the passenger door and attempted to ignore the approaching officers.

"Stay alert," Mathews reminded his partner.

They pulled up to the subject and cautiously exited their cruiser.

"Radio. Show us with one matching the description under investigation in front of 2358 23rd St.," Officer Mathews notified dispatch.

Using a non-intimidating tone, Officer Cooper asked the subject, "What's up man? What's going on?"

The subject stood there, still holding the bottle in his hand as if nothing was wrong; mistake number one. He then peered back over his shoulder towards the house he was standing in front of, smiled and raised both hands submissively into the air.

"Nothing Officer. Not a thing. I'm just out here chillin, sir," he smugly replied.

Mathews then asked the subject his name.

With that stereotypical technique that causes the brain to pause in order to come up with something, anything, he sadly answered, "Oh umm...me? Dre.", was what he decided to go with.

"Dre, could you put that bottle down for me?" Mathews requested, attempting to remedy mistake number one.

"Yes, sir. Absolutely. I don't want any problems," he said as he placed the bottle on the ground.

"Thank you. We appreciate that," Officer Mathews responded.

Still smiling, Dre replied, "I appreciate you. Both of y'all. I know your job is hard. I could never do what you do."

"Could you turn that radio down for me too?" Officer Cooper asked. "We got some complaints about it," he told him in an attempt to deflect blame and relate socially, as if he personally had no problem with the volume at all.

"My bad, Officer," he exclaimed as he leaned down into the vehicle to turn the radio down and the car off; mistake number two.

Realizing that they'd just sanctioned a possible dangerous outcome for themselves, Officer Cooper attempts to remedy mistake number two. He quickly walks up directly behind Dre as he stands back up. This is an offensive distraction tactic that occupies the subjects' thoughts while simultaneously minimizing space between two people. This smothering technique limits any possible offensive attack by the subject.

"It's okay. No problem, go ahead and put your hands on top of the car for me," Cooper instructed Dre.

"What I do?" Dre asked with confusion.

Now, with an ever maturing feeling of being harassed, disrespected and victimized, Dre became more and more upset as the investigation continued.

"Do you have your I.D. on you?" Cooper asked as he gave him a quick pat down for any weapons.

"For what? I ain't did nothin', Officer," Dre responded with a frustrated and aggressive tone.

Approaching from the opposite direction, Officer Tucker finally arrived to render his assistance. Tucker placed his scout car in park and updated Dispatch.

With no weapons found on Dre, Officer Cooper allowed him to stand back up and turn around.

"We just need your name for our log, stating that we talked to you and we'll be on our way," Mathews explained to Dre, hoping that he would stay calm and cooperative.

"Man, my name is DeAndre...DeAndre Smith", he told them. Pointing at the house he was standing in front of, he explained, "My I.D. is in the house. I live right there".

As Officer Tucker exited his scout car, he observed Dre's aggressive body language from a distance. He noticed an obviously mounting amount of irritation.

"Do me a favor, go grab your I.D. and we'll be out of your hair in no time," Officer Mathews requested.

"Fine, man. Can I go get it?" Dre asked.

"Yeah. We'll come with you. Go ahead," Cooper answered.

Officer Tucker began walking toward Officers Cooper and Mathews. Dre reached his front door and discreetly hurried in. Cooper and Mathews didn't notice Dre's sped up pace as the door closed behind him, but Tucker did.

Dre walked further into the house as Mathews and Cooper stopped and waited on the porch. Mistake number three. See, both officers thought they had no legal reason to enter the home once DeAndre entered. They were wrong, critically wrong.

"What's going on, Coop?" Tucker asked as he reached the porch also.

"He just went inside to get his I.D. right quick," Cooper casually replied.

"What?" Tucker shouted. Pointing out their potentially fatal mistake. Instantly switching to combat mode, Tucker ran up the porch steps, shoved both, Mathews and Cooper out of his way, and entered the house. He knew the typical mentality and culture that occupied the Delta area. He also knew that he had to do something, fast. They quickly followed him inside.

"You can't let the subject just walk in a house and you don't know what's inside," Officer Tucker scolded Coop and Mathews as he drew his weapon.

Just twenty feet away, they observed that DeAndre was about to enter an open bedroom door. He had just reached the first room down the long hallway when Tucker shouted, "Police! Don't move, or I will end you, right here," he warned.

Freaked out, DeAndre quickly put his hands up as he pleaded, "Wait wait! I didn't do anything. I was just getting my I.D. That's what he told me to do!"

But DeAndre was playing games.

"I don't care what that officer told you five minutes ago. You have a more, right now, kinda issue and if you move one more inch, I'm gonna introduce you to your ancestors," Tucker "politely" explained to Dre.

See, for all of the pleading and double talk, DeAndre hadn't stopped inching towards the room. Beginning to bend forward into the room, DeAndre tried to ask, "What do you mean? I..."

"Shut up and stop moving!" Tucker cut off his distracting plea. Warning again, as he carefully moved closer to DeAndre tightly aimed in.

"Ok ok ok." Dre muttered as he realized that his next decision would test his mortality's durability.

"Get him outta here," Tucker instructed Cooper and Mathews as they placed him in cuffs.

As Officer Tucker walks over to the open bedroom door, DeAndre yelled out, "You can't come into my house! Y'all ain't get my permission or a warrant."

Tucker looked in the room, and there it was. One step in the room and down in the corner there it was, itching for indiscriminate usage. A pistol grip twelve gauge Moss Berg pump; balanced there, leaning against the wall, fully loaded and ready.

"So you had intentions on killing us, huh Dre?" Mathews inquired with a building rage as he and his partner escorted DeAndre out to their scout car.

"Y'all wasn't supposed to come in my house anyway," DeAndre exclaimed. "I didn't say y'all could come in."

"I got news for you, Dre. We don't need your permission or a warrant. See, until we figure out who you really are and where you actually live, we don't know whose home this is. For all we know, you just broke in." Officer Tucker explained.

"You were gonna shoot us, Dre? Mathews asked again with a pulsating irritation.

"He was gonna try," Cooper confirmed.

"Nah, man...I wouldn't do that," DeAndre foolishly continued to explain.

"So what's your relation to the Jenkins family over here? And where's your I.D., Dre?" Cooper asked in a sarcastic tone.

"I don't know. It's somewhere in there," DeAndre replied.

"Who are you to the family?" Coop questioned.

"They're my cousins," Dre admitted.

"Well, cousin, we're gonna have to play adopt a name if we can't find your I.D. or confirm who you are," Mathews suggested.

In an anxious fear, DeAndre queried, "What does that mean?"

"We just want to know who we're talking to. As long as your record doesn't pop-up with a terrorist federal warrant, we can write you this ticket for the public drinking and like we said before you decided to take us on this ride, we can take the cuffs off and be on our way," Mathews explained.

Thinking to himself that he just needs to come clean and they would kick him loose, DeAndre decided to come clean and tell the truth so that he could get on with his day. Little did he know, Officer Mathews was still pissed at that idea of this guy trying to take his life.

Okay, Officer, my name is Anthony Duncan. I live on the next block, but the Jenkins are my cousins from my mother's side of the family. DeAndre is actually my uncle," Mr. Duncan finally revealed.

"Now that wasn't so hard. Was it?" Cooper rhetorically asked.

"You're on paper?" Officer Mathews inquired.

"Huh?" Duncan responded pretending to be clueless.

"Are you on paper? Parole?" Mathews questioned a second time.

With reluctance, Duncan replied, "Umm, yeah. I just got out. I just didn't want to go back there, Officer. That's why I told y'all that. My bad."

"We get it. That's not even on our radar right now. We just need the truth. Once we're done with running your name and giving you this coupon, you can go on home, up the street," Officer Mathews reassured him.

"Bet, thank you so much, Officer. I'll take the ticket, and again, I'm sorry for making your job complicated. And I wasn't gonna shoot anybody. I don't do that. You were just doing your job, that's all," Duncan replied.

Curious and not expecting an answer, Officer Cooper asked Duncan, "So where's your I.D.? It's not in the house is it?"

"Umm, no sir. I truly don't know where it is. I lost it a couple of months ago when I was outta town with my girl," Duncan answered.

"Yep, we figured that was a lie too," Cooper responded.

They entered Duncan's correct information into the system and bingo, "Surprise, surprise Mr. Duncan. The computer says that your parole is violated," Officer Mathews informed Duncan.

"It's not supposed to be. Oh, my P.O. told me to just call in the last time. She said that that would be good enough," Duncan replied.

Okay. That's cool. We're just gonna have to take you in and clear it up right quick."

Shocked, Duncan pleaded, "Nah, man. It's just a little mistake... You said if I told the truth that you would just write me a ticket and kick me loose."

"You know, you're absolutely correct, Mr. Duncan," Officer Mathews concurred. "But remember when you lied to us for twenty minutes straight?"

"Awe, naw, man. Officer, please," Duncan begged.

Neither officer had any true intentions on releasing Duncan. Instead, they implemented a tactic that allowed them to strategically retrieve the information that they needed to correctly identify Mr. Anthony Duncan; deception.

"Now you know how much you hurt our feelings," Cooper added.

Infuriated, Duncan convicted himself. "Man... the hell with both of y'all. Y'all dirty Bro! Y'all ain't even read me my rights! I shoulda went with my first mind and murked all three of y'all pigs!"

he blurted out, placing the final nail into his own coffin.

Narrowly saved from a number of consistent fatal mistakes by the intuition and experience of veteran Officer Tucker, Officers Mathews and Cooper arrested and transported Mr. Duncan to jail where he was unavoidably charged with home invasion, attempted murder, felon in possession of a firearm and issued a citation for the open container of intoxicant. With the help of in-car-video and the officers' testimony, Duncan was convicted on all charges and sentenced to eight to ten years, to be concurrently served.

-CONCLUSION-

In this case incident, many mistakes were made. Officers Cooper and Mathews were more concerned with identification and the legality of their investigation than their own safety. It was a good thing Officer Tucker arrived in enough time to prevent several potential fatalities. Using his experience and knowledge of the situation, area, and persons involved, he was able to employ the correct actions needed to maintain the safety of everyone involved.

In spite of the level of legal understanding that Officer Cooper and Mathews possessed at the time, the officers did have the right to enter the home, not just to verify Mr. Duncan's residence, but to confirm that there wasn't anything life threatening or illegal activity transpiring inside. Such as, the actual resident being tied up and incapacitated, or something even more sinister;

such as Mr. Duncan's heinous intention to unleash his devious ambush. And contrary to popular belief, there was no need for Mr. Duncan to be read his Miranda rights. He was not placed under arrest at the time and the officers were allowed to ask the initial identifying questions.

CHAPTER / seven

Morgan's Tactics

Natural enemies by proxy, criminals and police officers are constantly in a tug of war, jockeying for position. The constant mental battle between the two can be exhausting. Often expected to go above and beyond on a daily basis, this obligation can become psychologically traumatizing, but it also can become the highlight of their career.

Emotions routinely become real for officers during an investigation. For example, the feeling of helplessness can become more and more pronounced as he or she can only clasp on to the hand of the little girl in ICU. Victim of a stray bullet, her only sin was doing her homework in the front room of her own home. Or that moment where an officer tackles the malicious mind set of a deranged criminal, nauseously imagining the details, hoping to discover anything that could help apprehend a monstrous sycophant, guilty of several sexual assaults of elderly women. These are prime examples of circumstances that officers mentally enter into with the expectation of success and the ability to return psychologically intact. The keys to such success begins with tactics, a detailed form of skilled stratagem.

-CASE HISTORY-

It was late August. At its peak, the noon sun light is unforgiving. A physical and psychological war was taking place. At center stage was a distraught father, tightly gripping onto his four year old sons arm. Terror sets in as Officer Morgan received a run from dispatch.

"Three-Beat-One. Three-Beat-One. All cars in Three. We're getting Twelfth and Conner on a child neglect and possible suicide in progress. Caller says there's a man holding a little boy, sitting on the edge of a roof. The child is crying and the man appears to be upset. Three-Beat-One, cars in the Third precinct, that's Twelfth and Conner on a child endangerment, possible suicide."

"Three-Beat-One good and in route, Radio," Morgan responded.

Dispatch acknowledged Officer Morgan's response and assured him that the fire department was dispatched and would make the location also.

Officer Morgan activated his lights and sirens in an all-out race to the unthinkable. As he arrived, he observed the young, twenty something year old man sitting on the edge of a three-story building, with his legs dangling over the side. Morgan noticed a young boy seated in the obviously disjointed man's lap.

Officer Morgan notified dispatch. "Three-Beat-One, Radio. Show me at scene."

As Morgan exited his vehicle, the now obviously disturbed man shouted, "Stay away! Me and you ain't got nothing to talk about!"

Attempting to keep the situation calm, Morgan began implementing tactics. Tactic number one on his list was negotiations with recognition and compliance all to bring an intense posture down to a calmed place.

"You're absolutely correct. I just need to know if everything is ok?" Morgan replied.

"Everything is fine. Just leave me alone," the man told Morgan.

Sirens blazed loudly, intensifying as they got closer. Causing the situation to become even more dangerous.

"Radio, can you have the responding units kill their sirens. He's getting a little, too fidgety," Morgan asked dispatch. He then looked back up and replied to the man's request, "I would if I could but my boss told me to help you out."

"I don't need your help!" he angrily yelled.

Realizing that the man was still agitated and that the presence of the police failed to put pause to his reckless frame of mind, Officer Morgan ran through all the reasons of why this man could be upset and sitting on the top of a roof in such heat, holding a crying toddler. Is he upset about money? Maybe it's an employment problem. Could it be a family issue? Then it hit him, *"He's up there with his son. Where's the mother?"* Morgan thought to himself.

"That's your little boy, right?" Morgan decided to ask. "Where's the little fellas mom?"

The look on the man's face immediately turned to rage. "I don't know. You tell me. You probably know everything about her. You and your buddies are probably having a good laugh about it, huh?" he shouted out, as his grasp on the young boy became more and more careless by the moment.

At this point, Morgan's theory had been confirmed. He was angry with his significant other, the young boys' mother.

As back-up arrived with the fire department, Officer Morgan deployed tactic number two, proximity.

"Okay okay. Why don't I come up there, and we can sit and talk. Everybody doesn't have to know your business," Morgan suggested.

Then, the man showed his first sign of de-escalation. He paused with contemplation. "I don't need you to talk to me. You and me ain't got nothin' to talk about. Y'all leave me be," the man exclaimed.

Observing the crack in his armor, Officer Morgan quickly instituted his third tactic. "I know I know, but my boss, she won't let me go to lunch until you and I talk. She's irritating and freakishly nosey and my real boss put her in charge for today."

Morgan figured he'd play a sexist roll to show that they both had similar grievances. If his woman was his problem, then Morgan was gonna have an identical problem. Being on even ground where they could relate, gave an appearance of equal footing and understanding.

The man paused again. Before he could collect his thoughts, Morgan hit him with another question, "What's your name?" he queried.

The man hurriedly answered, "Brian, man."

"Brian. Okay, I'm Jimmy. Nice to know who I'm talkin' to. That's your boy? What's your boy's name?"

"James," he answered with an even more calming tone.

"Really? Same name as me, huh? It's a good strong name," Morgan replied as he was already thinking five steps ahead in the mortal chess match.

"I named him," Brian shouted with a sense of diluted pride.

"Of course of course. No female could understand that," Morgan continued. "Aye Brian, I'm gonna work my way up there right quick, but these other guys are gonna stay down here," Morgan dictated, taking yet another form of control away from Brian.

Brian hesitated. Instantly noticing his continuing reluctance, Officer Morgan began walking towards the old building as he simultaneously threw another thought at an already confused Brian. This was tactic number four. Morgan knew that the balancing act of steering the conversation and not allowing Brian to complete a thought, was vital.

The success of Morgan's forth tactic was based on the efforts of not allowing Brian to continue to have free will with his own thoughts and so far, it was working.

"Just so you and I can kick it for a minute," Morgan said, still gaining ground. "I'll help you out with your problem, we can get my supervisor off my back and then, maybe you and I can grab a quick bite when we're done, cool?"

Desperate to clear his head, Brian agreed. "Just you," he shouted with the misguided belief that he was still in control of the situation.

Morgan's forth tactic was a success. What Brian didn't know was that he had just gift wrapped what little control he still had and hand delivered it to Officer Morgan. Now, all Morgan had to do is take the rest.

Sweating bullets in the mid-summer heat, Morgan decided to violate department regulations and remove his vest as he makes his way through the condemned building. Chunks of wall and ceiling lay on the ground as he climbed the unstable stairwell.

"I'm almost there, Brian," Morgan shouted. "Jeez! How did you and James make it through all this?" he asked, as he remained engaged with Brian.

Officer Morgan finally made it to the roof and the truth of how hot it was, threatened his sanity. "Radio, Show Three-Beat-One on the roof with the subject," Morgan updated Dispatch.

Happy that he took his vest off to retain some sort of control over a pending heat stroke, Morgan knew he could use the one-hundred plus degree heat with his subliminal strategy.

"Damn, Brian. It's hot as hell up here!" Morgan exclaimed as he carefully walked across the tarred, shaky roof of the crumbling and fragile building.

Twenty feet away, Brian turned and shouted, "That's far enough. I can hear you from there," still holding on to James.

"Ok," Morgan answered as he surveyed the area around him. "Umm, Brian I know you and I just met, but I got two problems that I'm hoping you can help me out with."

"What, man?" he replied.

"Well, first thing is, I can just barely hear you from over here," Morgan explained.

"That sounds like a personal problem to me, Officer Jimmy," Brian responded with a tone of contempt.

"Ok, ok, I see," Morgan chuckled. "Well, my other problem is umm, this little piece of roof ain't gonna hold me too much longer; so I'm gonna have to make a move right quick, okay?" he continued.

With the sun beating down on his salty dehydrated skin and his son, James, scared and crying along with the onslaught of constant questioning, Brian's patience ran thin. "Fine, man," he exclaimed in a frustrated tone. "But don't come too close, or else I'm gone. Me and the boy!" Brian warned.

Though the threat birthed pause, Morgan had just implemented tactic number five. See, there was nothing wrong with where Morgan was originally standing. In fact, he was actually standing on the safest and sturdiest part of the tattered roof.

"I hear you," Morgan replied.

"Don't try me, man," Brian warned.

"Okay, I gotchu I gotchu," Morgan replied as he moved forward. "I'm just gonna come up about five or six more feet, okay?"

"Fine, but that's it," Brian responded as he turned back facing forward.

Morgan intelligently takes advantage of Brian's mistake, moving about twelve feet closer, instead. Closing the gap to now only eight feet.

"Is this good?" Officer Morgan asked in order to have Brian turn to see where his position was. This was done so that Brian wouldn't become upset with the new proximity.

Brian turned, "That's fine," he answered.

"Okay good," Morgan agreed as he brushed the dirt from his uniform. "Aye Brian. James looks a little thirsty. You want me to get some water up here?" he asked.

This was tactic number six.

"I don't want nobody else up here. I already told you," Brian shouted.

"No one else is coming up here. They can just throw it to me," Morgan reassured him.

Brian debated within his thoughts. He looked at his son. "Alright, man, get him a water," he said.

"You want one too?" Morgan asked.

Another moment of choice for Brian. Morgan understood that by asking if Brian wanted any water, it would call mortality to the forefront. See if Brian says yes to both him and his son having water, then he would more than likely be leaning towards survival and more importantly, he cared.

"Yeah, I'll take one too," he replied.

"Ok, cool. I'm just gonna walk up towards you a little so they can hear me on the ground, okay?" Morgan suggested, overloading Brian just enough.

Again, Brian's wheels go into overdrive, deciding on if Officer Morgan could move closer. "Just for the water and that's it. You can go back over there after that," Brian demanded.

Morgan agreed and began moving forward, "As a matter of fact, I'll ask them myself," Brian quickly suggested. "You just stay right there."

"No problem. Tell them to throw three up here," he told Brian, distracting him from the fact that he had just closed the gap to five feet.

As they await for the water to be thrown up to them, Morgan began tactic number seven, the gentle extraction of Brian's issues in a personal proximity.

Morgan got down on one knee and said, "Now that we're up here together, just us fellas. Give it to me, what's going on with you?"

"You're starting off all wrong, Bro. Don't act like you don't know, and don't come at me like I'm dumb!" Brian responded with a reinvigorated agitation.

Observing Brian becoming even more careless of how he was holding on to his terrified son, James, Morgan had to quickly move to his eighth tactic. A tactic where aggression is psychologically applied: the demand for answers.

Fearing that he could lose control of Brian's trust, Morgan quickly regained his psychological footing.

Aggressively, Morgan rattled Brian with his forceful tone. "Brian! I'm up here with you. I'm here for you. This is not just me doing my job anymore. I feel your pain, but you have to communicate with me. I've never met you before and I just got back to work yesterday, ok? I've been away and off for a while so you have to bring me up to speed on what you're talking about."

Causing panic for all of the first responders at the scene, Brian repositioned his body.

No, wait and *careful*, were the one worded sentences everyone shouted from below. Hoping for the best, and preparing for the worst, they fearfully waited on the ground.

Strategically returning back to a calmer demeanor, Officer Morgan quickly continued, "Now I noticed that you keep saying that we know what's going on and then you mentioned that we were laughing at you, but other than you and I talking about your lady acting up, I'm not clear on your specifics. Who is y'all and we, Brian? Help me help you, Bro."

"Shh...," Brian said to his son who was crying uncontrollably. Okay. I'll tell you."

"I appreciate that. But before we get started, let me get James to the Officers downstairs," Morgan suggested.

"No! He's staying with me!" Brian yelled emphatically.

Morgan quickly replied, "Okay. It's your world. I just didn't, you know, think he should hear our conversation. Especially if it's about his mother.

Not that I give a damn about her. I just don't wanna mess him up, you know?"

This was the moment Officer Morgan made his first mistake, and it turned out to be a huge one. See, he had unknowingly just pried his way into the meat of Brian's torment.

At the peak aggravation, Brian pulled out a six shot revolver and pointed it up in the air.

Morgan immediately stood to his feet. He placed his hand on his weapon, but realized that if he pulled his weapon out of his holster, the situation will more than likely end how Brian wanted it to originally end. With the death of him and his baby boy.

"Brian!" Morgan shouted.

All of the officers that were still on the ground immediately pointed their weapons at Brian and his son, now that Morgan and the rest of the first responder's lives were in jeopardy.

Holding his son even tighter now, Brian yelled, "Leave us alone!"

With his percentage of peaceful resolution dramatically dwindling, Morgan pled to Brian, "Brian. Put that thing down. It's not gonna help us here."

"There ain't no us!" Brian shouted aggressively as he turned his revolver on Morgan.

"Whoa, Brian!" Morgan exclaimed. "Wait!" he told him as he raised both hands and slowly moved to the edge of the roof. "Don't shoot," he shouted over the roof's edge to the other officers.

Brian gripped his son tighter, re-aimed his gun up into the air, and fired off a round. "Go ahead, shoot!" Brian angrily insisted.

"No!" Morgan yelled out. Knowing his life was in immediate peril, Officer Morgan pressed on. "Brian, hold on man. Look, you're scaring your son, man. You don't wanna do that. Let me give your boy to another officer and we can talk."

"Hmm. My boy, huh? I don't even know if he is mine. She played me for a fool. Sleeping around with everybody she ever walked past." Brian emotionally responded as the reality of everything began to kick in.

"That's what they do. But that's your son. Okay? You were the one who raised him. You gave him that powerful name. That was you Brian. You're the father, no matter what that slut did," Morgan said, attempting to convert Brian's thinking.

Divided, Brian loses his death grip on the building anger to the knowledge of what Morgan was saying. Regaining a fraction of control that he had only moments ago, Officer Morgan knew that he must repeat step one...relate.

"Brian, listen. I need you to give me the boy. I need James. He doesn't need to see this, Bro. Let me get James so that they can take him down stairs. He'll be right down there and you and I can talk about whatever you want to, ok? But you gotta put the gun away for me real quick. You can hold on to it for now. Just put it down for me, okay?" Morgan pleaded. "But I need you to give me James. I don't want those officers to get jumpy and start shooting up here, okay?"

With Brian still in thought, Morgan slowly reached for James, "Come on," Morgan calmly told James.

Distraught, Brian gradually began to realize what he was doing was wrong. He placed his weapon on the roofs ledge and carefully handed James over to Morgan.

Officer Morgan quickly carried the boy to the stairwell, handing him off to another officer. But he knew that his job wasn't over. He knew he had to now go back and accomplish the hardest part of this disturbing run. He had to convince this man that his life is worth living. If not for himself, then for his son, James.

"Brian," Morgan said as he cautiously returned back to that ledge. "Can I sit?" he asked.

With very little fight left, Brian replied, "Go ahead. Who cares? I'm done anyway."

Uncertain where Brian's thoughts now reside, Officer Morgan knew that now was the time to unarm him. Morgan instinctively unholstered his own weapon and replied to his disturbing comment, "No you're not."

He placed his pistol discretely under his thigh as he took a seat about four feet away from Brian. But Morgan's feet remained on the roof top, "Now that we got all that out of the way, I'm gonna need to get that gun you have over there, but please don't reach for it. Let me get it for you. I don't want any mistakes to happen after everything that we've been through. Is that okay?" he informed Brian, phrased as a question.

"I don't care anymore," Brian replied. "Do what you're gonna do."

Morgan reached over and safely picked up the weapon. Immediately, he turned his focus to talking Brian down, "Listen, believe it or not, you're not the only one this type of stuff happens to. She's not worth this much. Trust me, I know," Morgan explained to Brian.

Feeling completely defeated, Brian divulged the source of his depression. "She's been cheating on me with one of those detectives y'all work with over there."

Stunned, Morgan stuck to his game plan. "That's what you meant. Now I get it. I'm glad you gave me a chance to talk to you. Believe me, I get it, but it's time for you to man up," he said, issuing a challenge.

Brian looked over to Morgan with a tone of resentment.

"I'm telling you facts right now," Morgan continued. "Remember I told you that I'd been off work for a while? Well, I was out for about a week or two. Something similar happened to me."

This was Morgan's final tactic; the challenge.

"Officer Jimmy, you ain't got nothin' on me," Brian replied with a dangerously increasing depression.

Morgan chuckled, "Hmm hmm...you tell me. I think the last four months of my life may actually have everyone out here beat."

Morgan peaked Brian's interest, taking all the focus off of his finite intentions.

"Check this out, I get into an accident, tore my ride up and broke my foot. My wife cheated on me, and then left me. Then she took my son. I lost everything I own when my house caught fire and guess what, Brian? I'm still here, at work, wondering what the hell you're talking about. So what she cheated. There's thousands of women out there. Hell, my wife is out there. You're not alone Brian. And James is your son. You fed him. You clothed him. You raised him. That's your kid. Now come on let's go get something to eat. I'm still hungry," Morgan explained to Brian, blowing his mind.

After Officer Morgan's speech, Brian stood up and told Morgan, "My treat, bro. Keep your money. I'm sorry for you, you got issues. Let me help you downstairs."

Relieved, Morgan laughed as he and Brian both took the trek back down the frail stairwell, where Brian was placed into custody and transported to the crisis center for evaluation. Although Brian never got the chance to buy that lunch, he was eventually treated and released back into police custody where he was charged with multiple felonies including child endangerment. Eventually, Brian was able to visit his son...many years later.

-CONCLUSION-

Handled by a seasoned officer, and equipped with training, patience, understanding and a strategic plan, Officer Morgan effectively distracted, deescalated and disarmed the destructive circumstances. Using not only his training, Morgan was able to implement his own personal life, in order to save a life.

This is why officers must constantly balance their professional, and personal charge. Morgan was able to save multiple lives that day, but at what expense? An officer must be willing and ready to use every tool in their possession and sometimes, that may well include placing their own psyche in the line of fire, in order to achieve progressive results.

CHAPTER / eight

<u>No Time to be Neighborly</u>

There are days when it is imperative that police officers take a moment. A pause that allows the officer to reset his or her psyche. Unlike most careers, policing the free citizens of America is a challenge compared to only one other profession, a U.S. soldier. There are only two major differences between being a soldier and being a police officer. One, is the employer and the extent of the employers' authority. Both, soldiers and officers, police their assigned sectors, owning the responsibility of enforcing a policy to preserve order within a legal framework. The second difference is, the amount of exposure to the horrors of man. Unlike soldiers who are occasionally exposed to unimaginable sights when deployed into battle, police officers around the world are expected to experience very similar mind numbing atrocities on a daily basis, for decades.

Yet the rate of diagnosed PTSD remain polar opposites. Does this mean that it's expected that a police officer should be mentally stronger than a soldier? Or is it a blatant refusal to diagnose officers due to the cost? Sadly, it could also be that the officer is reluctant to admit that they are experiencing problems for fear of personal or professional reprisal. The fact that these identical traumas are treated differently, play a major part in maintaining the ability to fairly and effectively police a community.

-CASE HISTORY-

After months of painstaking hard work, Detective Penelope Lopez, assigned to the department's Violent Crimes Task Force Unit, was finally able to track down and arrest an individual that was wanted in several different states in connection with multiple unsolved homicides. A designated enforcer for an organization that was largely responsible for an illegal prescription pill epidemic that flooded a large part of America's mid-west.

In the course of conducting such a focused and intense manhunt for the fugitive, Lopez took some losses along the way. Positioned as task force command, the hundreds of decisions she made along the way came under fire. One in particular, burned deep inside and turned out to be more than she could bear. Her partner of four years, was sadly gunned down in the course of executing an arrest warrant towards the conclusion of the manhunt.

Although Detective Lopez was eventually and unequivocally cleared of all and any dereliction and incompetent conduct while in command, she continued to carry the heavy, backbreaking burden that seemed to be unrecoverable as it clawed its way deeper and deeper into her soul as time passed.

Ordered to take a well-deserved vacation, Detective Lopez realized the need to decompress. After weeks of seeing a department appointed counselor, Lopez needed a get-away moment. Finally, the day had arrived.

"YES! This is it! Today is the first day of my two week vacation," Lopez shouted with excited anticipation to herself as her alarm clock went off.

Little did she know, today would be the first day of the rest of her life. A life that would usher in a new outlook on the quality of living.

Although placed on modified duty, Lopez continued to burn the candle stick at both ends. After working the power shift with such of a consistent fortitude that would make the President of the United States commitment and work ethic look like an occasional stand-in favor, Lopez awoke, early that morning, packed her bags, picked up a couple of things from the store, and purchased her airline tickets to an island paradise somewhere in Hawaii.

It was ten o'clock in the morning of her heavenly trek and she had two last minute stops to make. As a single mother of two preteens, she was finally getting time to herself, on her dream vacation.

Immeasurably excited, she dropped off her two sons over to her mother's home before they headed off to school, "Okay guys, be sure to tell your grandmother you need to be at school by noon. Stay out of trouble and I love you," she told them.

A quick peck on the cheek and, poof... On to the next task before the ever awaiting tropical calm.

Only three houses away, she visited her neighbor and close friend, Bobby Boudreaux. Even though she always referred to him as Robert, Bobby was one of those neighbors that Penelope could always depend on. That one who would let her borrow that desperately needed cup of sugar, shovel the elderly neighbor's driveway, or even make a home cooked meal for Lopez's two sons whenever she couldn't make it home in time. Knowing that she was a single working mother, he also had somewhat of a colorful fondness for her.

With the kids on their way to school, she made her way over to Boudreaux's home. She knocked using her gentled civilian knock. She shouted, "Bobby, it's me, Penelope. Are you home?"

As if he were standing at the door awaiting her wondrous arrival, Bobby quickly opened his door.

"Hello there, Penelope. How you feeling today?" Bobby asked, grinning from ear to ear.

Startled at how fast the front door opened, Lopez stepped back. "Oh, hello there, Robert. I'm fine and yourself?" she answered and asked with a sense of exotic emphasis.

"I'm fine, now that you're here," he flirtatiously replied. "I see you're on your way, huh?" he continued.

"Yeah, I just wanted to make sure that you had everything that you needed. I gave you the keys already. Mikey and Steven will be over to their grandparents and don't forget about the lights and mail," she reminded him.

"Turn the lights on around eight and collect all your mail, right?" Robert confirmed.
"Exactly! You remembered. Thank you, Robert," She answered with a hint a flattery.

"Of course of course. Anything, anytime," he assured her.

"Okay, I'll make sure to remember that. And again, thank you for this. I really appreciate it. Maybe I can pay you back when I come home?" she suggestively suggested.

Shook, Bobby took a moment. As he imagined a moment with her, he agreed with her proposal. "I'd like that."

"It's a date! Say, do you know when they will be done with that construction going on next door to you?" she asked.

"No, unfortunately. They've been at it at all types of hours for days now. They keep the whole neighborhood up with that racket," Bobby answered.

"I'll put a call in to the city for you. Maybe that will put an end to the after hour noises," Penelope suggested.

"That would be amazing." he replied.

"No problem. I'll call you when I land," Penelope assured him.

They gave each other an intimate hug and bade each other farewell.

"Penelope, now you know you can't get on that plane with your gun still hanging off of your waist like that, right?" Bobby told Lopez, noticing the hard bulge blocking his hand at the small of her back.

She smiled and let out a chuckle as she turned to walk away and told him, "No, I'm gonna drop it off at the station on the way." Still smiling, she jests, "But if they frisk me anywhere near as good as you just did, there's no telling what they might find."

Laughing, Bobby wished her safe travels as he waved good bye.

Walking back past the loud home that was under construction, towards her luggage stuffed Jeep, Lopez heard shouting coming from a house directly across the street from Bobby Boudreaux's home. Without breaking a stride, she peered over her shoulder and saw a shirtless irate man, hanging halfway out of the front second floor window of his house, screaming at the top of his lungs. She couldn't quite clearly hear exactly what he was saying, so she forced her instinct to disregard the confusion and remain focused on her vacation.

Just as she reached her jeep, she heard a loud, "bang"...

Still stressed, Lopez flinched then she realized it was just the very loud and clumsy construction workers dropping pallets of wood onto the ground.

With a sense of relief and a bit of embarrassment, Lopez let out a sigh.

She opened her front passenger door and threw her one last bag onto the seat. But as she closed the door back, she heard another loud bang. Unfazed, she reluctantly turned to look. But as she turned, she noticed that the shirtless man across the street was now holding an assault rifle, pointing it directly at her.

Just as he fired, life must've hit the slow motion button because her brain told her to move, but she still experienced every bit of that moment as if it were a movie played out frame by frame.

First the flash from the muzzle, then an unmistakable, "bang" in course with a whizzing sound that the bullet made as it buzzed right by her ear, shattering her passenger side rearview mirror.

Shocked, Lopez ducked. "Oh shit!" she exclaimed with panic. She pulled her weapon out and quickly took cover, diving down onto the ground on the passenger side of a car that was parked at the curb in the street.

"GET DOWN! SOMEBODY, CALL NINE-ONE-ONE!" Lopez shouted to the construction workers.

Unable to hear her plea over the loud construction, two workers are struck by the deranged shirtless assassin. It was only then that the other workers realized what was actually transpiring.

As they took cover, Lopez realized that the man was mainly targeting the construction crew. "He must be pissed at them," Lopez thought to herself.

Still stunned, she yelled, "POLICE!", as she aimed her weapon at the unwitting sniper, firing three shots,
But she missed.

But it caught his attention. An attention she had not intended to intentionally attract.

The gunman thought he had easy pickings as he turned his murderous rage to Lopez. He knew he had her out gunned and he focused all of his efforts into killing her for getting in his way and firing shots at him.

What the shirtless sniper didn't know, was that the three shots that Lopez had just fired, successfully missing him, was more lucky for him, than he could have ever imagined. See, Lopez wasn't always, just a detective. Prior to making a commitment to her community, she made a commitment to her country. Serving two tours as a U.S. Marine bad-ass, Penelope Lopez successfully attained the rank of captain, where she became one of the first few females ever to qualify as a tier two operator. Tearing down every barrier along the way, she eventually earned the reputation as that one female soldier known to embarrass her male counter parts, regularly. Specifically for this narrative, the expert pistol and rifle shooting skills she acquired in her time of active service will be the particular.

The sniper continued to fire relentlessly. Rapid shot after shot, he fired tearing rabid holes that riddled the parked car that Lopez took cover behind.

Realizing that she only had one chance at taking this guy out, Lopez quickly regained her wits and snapped into her trained survival mode. She now knew what she had to do and that was simply to stay patient.

Moving from the front of the vehicle where the engine block protected her, she discretely crawled her way to the trunk area, exposing herself to a higher risk of being struck by the high powered rifle. But she needed to be sure he didn't see her, so she moved smartly.

Needing to see exactly when the deranged trigger-man would need to duck back into the house to reload, she waited for the pause in his malicious melee. Then, it happened, he blinked.

Lopez cautiously peeked out from her cover, it was clear. She took her one chance and sprinted lowly to the construction company van that was also parked on the street, just behind the car she first used as a shield, where she waited.

The enraged man popped his head up, aimed in, and lit that poor vehicle up, but it was the wrong vehicle. He had no idea that she had changed her position.

Determined, the crazed man decided to come down from his tower of terror in order to confirm the validity of his work, accompanied by the hope of revel.

With an eerie sense of calm, he eagerly walked down his stairs from the upper rooms to his front door and casually opened it. Barefoot and dressed in only a pair of dirty blue jogging pants, he took a dramatic stance within his doorway as if he were taking in a well-deserved ovation. He inhaled, enjoying a deep breath, sharpening his focus. The rifle raised high; pointing the business end sharply into the air. He then reloads his weapon as he stepped off onto his front porch with an evil determination. With a smile, the sniper moved in.

Walking at a focused pace, his tunnel vision took over as he lowered the muzzle, racked a round into the chamber and aimed in. Just as his feet touched the streets pavement, he opened fire again. Dumping round after round after round into that same unfortunate vehicle, but again, it was the wrong vehicle.

Lopez immediately saw his fatal mistake. Now in his blind spot, she tactically abandoned her cover. She took in a deep breath. "POLICE!" she shouted.

Only thirty feet away, he turned, swinging the high powered rifle towards her position. Without taking any more chances, Detective Lopez utilized her training, instantly finding her target, and firing until the threat was no longer a threat.

Detective Lopez ended the rampage with two shots, striking him once through the bridge of his nose and once through the center of his chest.

The aftermath left two construction workers injured, one tattered car, and an immeasurable psychological ripple effect. After further investigation, it turned out that the extremely disturbed middle aged man hadn't been taking his psychiatric medications and was suffering from a case of sleep deprivation due to the odd hours that the construction company kept. Records showed that, for days, he called 911 and became even more frustrated that it continued; even with the help of the police responding. He'd finally decided to take matters into his own hands with the obvious intentions on fixing at least one of his problems that morning.

-CONCLUSION-

This situation involved an off duty officer that quickly found out that an officer is never actually really off duty. Although allowed time to recover from a psychological battle, an officer can never completely let their guard down. This is a fact that will burrow its way into their life's nature, forever.

Although this hard learned mentality can prove to be rewarding and effective, it is neither natural nor healthy for the human brain to constantly remain in such a heightened state of combat readiness. This mindset personality can easily become damaging, causing many issues such as unintended aggression, nightmares and violent out bursts while asleep. It can also put a strain on both personal and professional relationships during and after an officer's career.

This is why it is imperative that officers, soldiers and anyone dealing with any form of psychosis, PTSD or any other kind of mental illness, seek and receive proper medical help. This type of mental stress coupled with the effect of losing a life or taking a life can prove to be catastrophic. Left unchecked, these psychological cancers can slowly eat away at a life, dismantling any kind of peaceful normalcy.

CHAPTER / nine

No Good Deed...

There will come a time in everyone's life when they will have to make a split decision that may embody an instantaneous effect with finite results. But in the career of an officer, those moments in time will multiply exponentially. This is why it is important for every officer to accept and understand that every action that they take while in service of the community, may at times, whether it be good or bad, go beyond their intentions. It is the sacrificial plunge that is assumed in all law enforcement.

-CASE HISTORY-

It's nine o'clock in the morning. Officer Roderick Parker awakes to an eerie feeling. As if it were a tap on his shoulder, the twelve year veteran with great instincts had a feeling that something big was going to happen that day.

Working scout Ten-Twenty-One in the special operations' plain clothes unit, he and his partner, Officer Erica Cook, were pounding the city streets in search of the local neighborhood B&E man. Midway through their grueling twelve hour shift, they decide to pull into a gas station to grab a quick snack.

"I'm starving. You coming in?" Parker asked.

"Yep, I could go for a quick snack," Cook replied.

As the officers exited their vehicle to go inside, they encountered a young man.

"How are you doing today officers?" he asked as he reached to open the door for them.

"Good," Cook answered. "And yourself?"

"I'm fine, Officer. Just enjoying the day," he replied.

Just that quick, Parker's notorious instincts kicked in. See, the young mans' demeanor was strange. He had already performed the infamous hesitation move, where his brain told him to walk away as soon as he saw the scout car, but then suddenly changed his mind in an effort to maintain his cool and act natural. Added to the fact that he was too chatty and obvious with his intent to distract them from whatever else he was really doing, he had unknowingly already given himself away.

Parker decided to ignore the fact that the man was just standing in front of the entrance appearing to have no other kind of business up there. For all he knew, the young man could have had an arrangement with the owner to clean up the grounds around the property. Uncertain,

Parker continued on his mission for sustenance to put some distance between his stomach and his spinal cord.

While inside, the store clerk whispered to the officers, discretely telling them that the man who opened the door to let them inside, had been hanging around outside in the parking lot harassing his customers all day. The clerk went on to describe the unknown man as aggressively refusing to leave. It was at that point that Officer Cook decided to handle the situation with a terminating resolution.

Cook and Parker finished their purchase with the hope that the young man would've been smart enough to have left the area by the time they came out. But you know what they say, "Criminals come in all kinds of dumb."

Both officers exited the store, and sure enough, there he still stood. As he awkwardly tried to avoid eye contact, Officer Cook goes in on him, "Aye, guy? What's up? Why are you all of a sudden avoiding us?" Officer Cook inquired.

"Who, me?" he asked with confusion written on his face.

"Who me? That's mistake number one...and this ain't baseball either. Yeah, I'm talking to you and there's no such thing as a third mistake," Cook responded with a tone of agitation.

Parker quickly surveyed any path of possible escape for the now panicking young man. Discretely, Officer Parker positioned himself just out of sight, behind the left shoulder of the subject as Cook continued to make him sweat.

"I haven't done anything," he replied.

"Exactly. We've been in and out of there and you're still up here. Why are you up here?" Cook asked him as if they didn't already suspect the true nature of his loitering.

"I'm working. They let me clean up for a couple of dollars," he claimed.

"Yeah, nope. Bye. He doesn't want you up here," Cook advised.

"But..."

Parker cut him off. "You shoulda got lost when we gave you the chance, Bro. You just made mistake number two. Let me see some identification please."

In a stage of pure fear, the foolish young man makes a horrible decision to glance upward, looking past the officers in an attempt to find that ever illusive escape route.

Parker quickly warned him, "Son, I'm telling you now. If you do it, I promise you, you will spend the rest of today and most of tomorrow regretting it as you count the ceiling tiles from the bed in your hospital room."

Knowing he was done for, the young man simply gave up, put his hands on the wall and willfully divulged all his information.

"Shit! Man, I don't have my I.D. on me right now Sir. But my name is Andre Fuller, Officer," he reluctantly admitted with an almost unbearable amount of frustration.

As Officer Parker continued to conduct his routine "Terry stop" pat down for "dangerous weapons", Officer Cook checked the data base on the computer and quickly discovered that the young man had a misdemeanor traffic warrant. The pat down of Mr. Fuller's outer pant pockets didn't reveal any obvious suspicious weapons, but he did notice a couple of significantly hard pebble sized crumbs freely rolling around in one of the pockets though.

Cunningly, Officer Parker decided not to share that bit of information with him just yet.

"You stay over on East Braile Street?" Officer Cook inquired in order to help confirm Mr. Fuller's correct identity.

"Yes Ma'am," he answered.

"What's the numbers?" she further inquired to validate if the numbers matched or not.

He gave her the correct numbers and after a few more questions, it's official; it's Mr. Fuller.

Now the type of misdemeanor warrant that popped up allows officers to use his or her own discretion in the decision to arrest or advise and release.

Both officers decided together to go ahead and place the young man, now known as Andre Fuller of East Braile, under arrest. But before they actually did, they made sure that he knew that they could.

"We gotta little problem, Andre. The computer says that you have a warrant out of Anderson County," Officer Cook advised him.

"Awe, man. Naw, Officer, I took care of that last month," Fuller explained to Officer Cook.

Just in case Andre was the actual B&E man that they had been looking for, Cook and Parker use their leverage to get a little information out of him.

"That's not what my digital girlfriend says here. She told me that someone wanted at least a thousand dollar piece of you," Parker responded, referencing the price on a county warrant.

Careful not to actually tell Fuller that he was under arrest, Cook asked, "Do you have anything on you that I should know about? Tell me now," she warned.

"This is your chance. If we get down there and we find something on you, then it's yours and there's nothing we can do about it," Officer Parker added to his partner's well advised cautioning.

"Go ahead and empty out your pockets," Cook "encouraged" Fuller.

Remembering the "Terry stop" pat down, Officer Parker eagerly encouraged Fuller to empty everything out of his pockets. See, it became obviously clear to Parker that Mr. Fuller had no clue of what was still in his pocket. Possibly thinking that he had already gotten rid of whatever stash he had, Fuller continued to bare whatever remained in his possession.

"Come on, flip them pouches," Parker hurried Fuller.

The extremely helpful and cooperative self-administered inventory search of Fuller's pockets eventually revealed exactly what Parker's intuition and experience told him, Andre Fuller was holding.

Just as he placed his hand inside of his pocket one last time he felt it. "Oh shit!" Fuller thought to himself as his fingers rolled across the top of the plastic that was tightly tucked away deep inside his pockets. It was the last three small baggies of his crack cocaine.

Well under the felonious amount, the suspected crack cocaine was good enough for a ticket and an additional misdemeanor charge, but again, the resolution of this additional charge can also be decided by the officers. They could arrest or confiscate the suspected drugs, or confiscate the suspected narcotics, issue a misdemeanor ticket and then release him, but which one?

"Let's go ahead and hook him up and get some prints on him, just in case," Officer Parker suggested to Cook.

"Sorry, Bro. You gotta few issues that need taken care of. So umm, you're gonna have to spend the rest of the day with us," Parker so eloquently explained.

Realizing that he should have taken the helpful advice to leave the first time, the young man made one last attempt to free himself, "Ok, ok, I'mma leave. Just, please, don't take me to jail. I was just trying to make a little money. I got kids," he pled.

"Why you gotta bring the kids in this?" Parker asked menacingly. "You gotta take this like a man."

As the truth began to sink in even more, the only response he had was, "You right, man. My bad. I'mma stop talking now."

Cook and Parker, both laughed.

"Good idea," Officer Cook happily agreed.

As Officer Cook copied down the information from the computer and began to fill out her misdemeanor citation, an urgent call for help came out over the radio.

Priority, Radio Ten-Two. We got one running eastbound from Third and Franklin. He's headed towards Grand Boulevard on foot!" They managed to transmit in a heavy breath as they pursue, also on foot.

Officer Cook and Parker's attention immediately focused in on the officer's call for help.

"What's the description and what are you chasing for, Ten-Two?" Dispatch asked.

Obviously running out of breath, they manage to respond, "Clean shaven Hispanic male, five foot-nine, white shirt, blue jeans, red shoes, Radio. It's a homicide suspect and he just crossed over to Grand Boulevard headed north."

Realizing that the perp was headed directly for them, Parker's instinct kicked in. "We gotta kick him, Erica," Parker decidedly suggested.

As Fuller was only detained and never officially arrested, Cook promptly agreed, "You just lucked out, Bro," she said as they make an executive decision to exercise their discretion.

"We're gonna give you this coupon and advise you the you have a seventh district misdemeanor warrant that you need to take care of. Now bounce, Bro," Officer Parker instructed the now fortunate young man.

"Thank you, thank you, thank you!" He gratefully repeated.

"You can go now, just stay from up there," Cook told him as she handed him his ticket.

They hurriedly take off diving head first into the chase. "Radio. Show Ten-Twenty-One in the area, around the corner. Parker notified dispatch. Is he still heading north?" he asked.

"Where are you now, Ten-Two?" Dispatch wondered.

"Still northbound on Grand Boulevard, approaching Brighton," they responded.

Officer Cook informed Dispatch. "We see them. We're pulling up on them now, Radio."

Parker skid to a halt as Cook jumped out of the car. Scout Ten-Two was too far behind him. They couldn't catch up.

"Police! Stop!" Officer Cook yelled as the fleeing perp decided to take a short cut through a funeral home.

Parker drove into the packed parking lot, but is cut off by construction work being done on the lot and adjoining sidewalk in the rear of the building.

Unable to continue pursuit using the scout car due to the obviously ongoing and heavily attended funeral, Officer Parker quickly threw the car in park and jumped out.

"I'mma go through the back, to the other side!" he shouted to his partner."

Separated, he'd hoped that his instincts were spot on with the decision to not follow his partner and the perp through the funeral home. See, Parker had this unshakable intuition that the perps impulse to enter the unwitting business was only to cut through it, in order to gain more distance for his escape. Somehow, Parker knew that the subject was definitely coming out on the other side of the building, he just had to get there.

As Officer Parker turned the corner of the building, he was met by five construction workers working in the lot. As he reached the second corner, he saw one worker standing on the sidewalk smoking a cigarette.

"You see anybody come through here?" Parker hurriedly asked the construction worker.

"Nah," he casually replied.

"Radio, can I get a location on my partner?" Parker asked, second guessing that earlier decision to separate from Cook.

"He's coming out the side door now," Officer Cook shouted in her transmission through her radio.

Officer Parker turned to run up the sidewalk to the side door. He takes about six or seven strides, and then as if the building gave birth to pure evil intentions, the perpetrator's arm suddenly extended outward from a brush covered recess in the wall, pointing assured death directly at Officer Parker.

Perilously shook, Parker stopped in his tracks. His nerves momentarily paralyze his body. Only inches from his head, Officer Parker became unnaturally intimate with every click and pause of every gear and mechanism within the handheld cannon.

Then, a sound that wields the power to tear a whole in reality itself. The empty echo of cold metal snapping against cold metal. "Click."

A biblical and miraculous misfire...

The perpetrator retracted the gun into his stomach as he struggled in an attempt to rack a new round into the chamber.

Parker quickly turned, exposing his back in order to reach out for the innocent construction worker in an attempt to shield him from what was about to happen.

The perpetrator immediately aimed in and two shots rang out. One shot struck Parker in his vest, directly in the center of his back. The second shot hit him in one of the few places that a bullet resistant vest did not protect, his left shoulder where the elastic strap connects to the actual vest.

The impact force from the rounds that struck Officer Parker in the back, added to his momentum, causing him to fall forward, tackling the construction worker to the ground. Unfortunately, the heroic move caused both of them to land on top of Parker's right hand, his shooting hand. The weight and force from the fall shattered the bones in two of the fingers in his shooting hand.

Although badly injured, Parker knew he had to make some kind of move, immediately. As the perp relentlessly walked towards the now wounded officer, it was apparent that he approached with the intent to finish what he had begun, but once again, his handgun misfired.

Somehow, Parker rolled over onto his left side, gripped his weapon with his mangled right hand and yanked his weapon from the holster. With lives on the line, Officer Parker endured the excruciating pain as he quickly aimed towards the immediate threat headed his way.

With no potential unintended victims in the line of fire, Parker discharged his weapon. He was able to get off five shots with two broken fingers and bleeding from a bullet that was lodged somewhere in his shoulder, Officer Parker missed his fifth shot, but utilized his first four effectively. In a progressive upward pattern, he was able to strike the perpetrator four times.

The perp immediately stopped his aggressively murderous advance. Now seriously injured, he paused. That's when Parker intuitively made his own tactical move. Still aimed in at the perpetrator, Officer Parker knew that he needed to put a significant gap between himself and the deranged agent of death. He quickly stood to his feet, "Stay here and stay down," he told the construction worker.

The perp began firing again. Still severely wounded, Parker switched gun hands. With each bullet whizzing by, narrowly missing, Officer Parker tactically retreated backwards as he politely continued to introduce his remaining live rounds to the fleeing outlaw.

With one trying to murder the other and the other trying to stop the murderer, Parker emptied his weapon, firing the last ten rounds in his magazine, striking the perp four additional times.

Riddled with bullet holes, the felon immediately collapsed.   Parker dropped to his knees, struggling to remain conscious. Just as the mayhem concluded, Cook exited the building with her gun drawn. Seeing that the perpetrator and Parker were down, she quickly retrieved the subject's weapon as she ran past him and immediately checked on her partner.

"Shit! Hot Rod, are you okay?" she asked in a panic.

"He got me," Parker exclaimed, writhing in pain. "Make sure he's okay," he continued, worrying more about the construction worker than himself.

Still in shock, the worker quickly resolved Parker's concern. "I'm fine, Officer. Shit, you saved me. Are you okay?"

"Radio! My partner is hit. Officer down. We need E.M.S. at Grand Boulevard and Franklin. He's still conscious. Radio, the perp is down also. It's unknown on his status," she relayed over the air.

Unable to attend to, both her partner and the perpetrator, Cook stayed with her partner until help arrived.

Moments later, Ten-Two arrived at the scene and attended to the injured subject until the ambulance made the location and rendered aide.

Though, shot a total of eight times, the emergency measures used by the officers, ambulance and hospital personnel were enough to keep the fleeing armed bandit alive. Although, he probably wished that he'd died. See, Parker's fight to stay alive caused permanent medical issues for the armed felon. One bullet hit him in the knee, destroying it completely. The second bullet struck him in the scrotum, obliterating his left testicle. The third and fourth one tore through his bladder, forcing him to wear a urine bag for the rest of his life, the fifth and sixth fragmented in his left lung, causing too much damage to save...and the seventh and eighth bullet ripped through his shoulder and collar bone, crippling the joint for life.

Turns out, Ten-Two received a tip on a subject with a homicide warrant hanging out at a carwash. Once they made the location, the suspect quickly sped off. The armed assailant was immediately pursued where he intentionally t-boned a scout car injuring the officers. He then fled on foot where he eventually was introduced to Officer Roderick Parker.

After confirming that the suspect was wanted in connection with two open murders, a more thorough investigation revealed that the gun used to shoot Officer Parker, was registered as stolen. Consequently, the gun evidence and fingerprints helped to determine that the swift footed shooter was in fact, none other than the neighborhood B&E bandit that Parker and Cook had been frustratingly searching for, during the last few weeks.

-CONCLUSION-

This event shows how officers, when permissible, have to utilize their own prerogative when a situation presents a demand for it. But the most important take away of the story, is the intuition of a seasoned officer. Equipped with experience knowledge and a little luck, that gut feeling should not be dismissed so easily. It can sometimes be the difference between life and death.

Having good instincts is only the start. The success of good police work boils down to one thing, information. The lack of information can contribute to avoidable complexities that can compound in a very short amount of time, placing unnecessary jeopardy on all responding officers. It is imperative to communicate all pertinent information in order to effectively enforce the law.

From wrongful incarceration to an avoidable fatality, without good and accurate information, anything can happen. An officers' decision making based on good information is imperative to surviving law enforcement.

Kristopher W. Allen

CHAPTER / ten

Subvert: to *social media*

The term, **subvert** [*suh* b-**vurt**], is a verb meaning to undermine the moral principles of (a person, etc). To corrupt or cause the downfall, ruin, or destruction of. Social media can easily be used as a subversive tool; or in this case, a weapon.

Just as any other frustrated being on this planet, sometimes officers suffer from the heaviness and hardships that are randomly introduced into their lives, daily. After a while of being subjected to a constant bombardment of both internally and externally generated problems, emotions can build, distorting patience, empathy and understanding. This reaction can be expressed in many different ways. An uncontrollable release of those emotions can present itself with or without rationale.

A road often taken that routinely produces a tolerable sense of satisfaction, is venting. Venting is the act of giving release or discharge through expression of thought and or emotion. Sometimes, sharing the grievance can help more than just the person whom it was actually meant for. Sometimes that therapeutic vent can be just the right thing needed for that unsuspecting individual.

This is an example of an agent in law enforcement that decided to exercise his or her first amendment by educating each reader while administering a much needed type of self-piloted therapy by either sharing someone else's post, or expressing their own thoughts and emotions utilizing a popular social media platform.

-CASE HISTORY-

Scenario:A

Officer Kimberly Forman

I'm not sure who wrote and posted this, but everybody should read this.

-"Before you judge one of us, remember this,

Those who fight monsters inevitably change. Because of all that they see and do, they lose their innocence, as well as a piece of their own humanity. If they want to survive, they begin to adopt the mindset of a monster, absorbing the poisonous characteristics as those same monsters that they fight. Now, born of necessity, they consequently become capable of rage, and extreme violence.

However, there is a fundamental difference. Cursed with the charge of such corruption, we must keep those monstrous tendencies locked away in a cage, deep inside. That monster is only allowed out to protect others, to accomplish the mission, and to get the job done. Never for the perverse pleasure that the actual monsters feel when they harm others. In fact, those monstrous tendencies can contribute to the damage regularly experienced. Damage like, guilt, isolation, depression, and PTSD are among many of the mental and social challenges that accompany this ill-mannered behavior.

There is a cost for visiting violence on others when your first nature is not of a monster. Those who do so know one thing; the cost inflicted upon society as a whole is far greater without those who fight monsters. That is why they are willing to make such a heavy sacrifice...so that others may live peaceably.

We are witnesses to the things that humans aren't meant to see, and we see them repeatedly. We perform the duties that you feel are beneath you. We solve your problems. We intentionally run towards the things that you intentionally run from. We fight what you fear. Sometimes under the call or demand of visiting violence upon others, we stand between you and those monsters that desperately want to harm you. You want to pretend that they don't exist, but we know better. We do the things that the vast majority are too weak or too scared to do.

We believe that fighting for others is honorable, noble, and just...and we are willing to pay the price for that deeply held belief. Why? For us, it isn't a choice. It is what we are. We are simply built that way.

So remember, before you judge us, it is because of that selfless sacrifice, that your life is more peaceful."

- Unknown Author

119 Commented - 915 Shared

 Kathleen Wyatt

-"Bravo. Well said. Those who believe that monsters don't exist are fools. Those that fight the monsters are the gate keepers that we need. I believe there are more warriors than we know and that gives me hope and strength. I'll pass this along to remind us of what we have inside us; the will to fight for right and to always thank the gate keepers.

With multiple reactions and comments to these posted ideas, discussions quickly become a kind of justification for the root issue. Whatever the original statements made, it proves to provide support for the topic at hand, shedding light on the fact that there is more than just the original author of the post that carry interests with said topic.

Although this process can, at times, provide a much needed mental release from pressure, it can also prove to become a honeytrap. If used incorrectly, social media platforms can breed the opposite effect. Effectively destroying lives and careers.

S c e n a r i o : B

Officer Ronda Hartford

-"Another night trying to wrangle in these zoo animals."

3,019 Commented - 13,015 Shared

Reggie Bowman

-"This is the kind of officers that we have protecting us?"

Jennifer Richmond

-"WTF?"

Kevin Jamison

-"Where does she work? I never want to

have an encounter with her."

Jorge Gonzalez

-"That's exactly why I don't like the police."

Mimi Anderson

-"She needs to be fired. I can't stand pigs."

With even fewer words, placed in a certain order and spoken at a time in society where certain particular choice words usher questionable intent, those who utilize social media without thought, effectively expose themselves, becoming a target. Gestures, statements, gifs and memes can easily become twisted and misunderstood, just as they can be enlightening, revealing ones' character.

Although free speech is an established constitutional right, it is incumbent of an officer to use good judgment when utilizing any kind of social media. Law enforcement is an authoritative entity that represents a larger form of government. A government that is empowered and formed by the people, for the people, and of the people. Therefore issues of beliefs, personal thoughts or ideas, and feelings toward all subjects, whether it be made as an enlightening or playful statement, should be accompanied with consequential thought. Captions, quotes and comments can go in three very different directions. Either they will be ignored, applauded or outraged from the shared content.

In this particular instance, the shorter statement in scenario B carried more charged wording than the much longer social media post in scenario A. Without further insight on what the second officer meant, her statement gave birth to an uncontrollable wave of social media backlash, calling for her removal as an officer. Consequentially, Ronda Hartford was charged with conduct unbecoming an officer, bordering dereliction of duty. Ultimately, she was eventually dismissed from her oath of practicing law enforcement with that particular city.

But why?

What does her statement mean and how many ways can it be interpreted? Is it said jokingly? Is it said as a characterization of the type of mentality, antics and or situations of the people that she polices on a daily basis? Or, maybe, just maybe, this officer is mentally bombarded with so much personal emotion, that she let a flawed and unexpected part of her, otherwise repressed, personality slip.

Freudian or not, while communicating with others within any capacity, face to face, news media, social media or via telephone, all officers should consciously refrain from placing themselves in any kind of compromising position, possibly exposing themselves to be persecuted and even prosecuted, both professionally and or personally.

-CONCLUSION-

In short, communications used by any representative of a government, corporation or any other kind of a publicly dependent organization in today's societal multi-dysfunctional state, should exercise extreme caution with all media outlets due to the heavy checks and balances of public perception.

CHAPTER / eleven

The Diabolical Doppelgänger

As an officer, there will be times when it is important to look beyond what's in front of you. The balancing act between fact and fiction lies within the ability to sift through the intentional deception and single minded tunnel vision. The following case illustrates a prime example of how an investigating officer utilizes their imagination, logic and evidence to generate a complete picture of events that, more than likely, took place in the commission of a crime.

-CASE HISTORY-

Geared up for the start of a new day, Officer Steven Harper heads in to work knowing that he volunteered for an extra shift. The plan was to work his regular morning shift, and then stay for the afternoon. The problem with that was, he thought he would be fine working sixteen hours straight. But what he didn't know, was that his sixteen hour day was about to turn into a twenty-five hour bad, now you see me now you don't, murderous magic trick.

Officer Harper worked his first eight hours flawlessly. Absent of any hiccups, Harper had successfully made it through his regularly scheduled shift and was poised and ready to start his overtime tour. Although Officer Harper had been experiencing an average type of a Thursday, the sun soon would decide to make its final curtain call midway through his extended work day, giving birth to the city's monsters of the night.

Working scout Nine-Two, Officer Harper and his partner, Rachelle Banks were out patrolling the summers' hot evening city streets when they heard a priority run dispatched over the air.

"Cars in District Nine, cars in District Nine. We're getting one down. One down near the corner of Shelby and Hayes. Caller says that the victim is her friend and that she can't wake her up." Dispatch read off in a general announcement for any unavailable unit to volunteer for.

Hearing the nature of the run, Harper and Banks quickly answer the call to service. Officer Banks grabbed the radio mic, "Nine-Two in route. We're about five minutes out," she replied.

"Nine-Two, I show you heading that way. EMS says they're about fifteen minutes out," Dispatch responded. "Nine-Two, I have some additional information here. We're also getting a couple of calls of shots heard fired in that area around the same time. Be advised; these runs could be related. Use caution," Dispatch advised.

Other available units begin to also answer up in an effort to back-up Nine-Two with this breed of potentially dangerous police run.

"Show Nine-Eleven making the scene, Radio."

"Nine-Nine on the way also."

"Nine-Five in route, coming from the north, Radio."

"I show Nine-Eleven, Nine and Five making the location for an assist to the corner of Shelby and Hayes on an unresponsive one down. The run should be coming across your screens now. Let me know if anyone needs a repeat on the circumstances?"

As all four responding police units continued to make their way to the scene, the dispatcher updated them with a new time of arrival for the ambulance.

"Nine-Two...Nine-Two and the additional responding units, be advised. EMS is delayed coming from another medical run." Dispatch announced.

Running lights and sirens blazing, Harper and Banks hit the corner at Shelby and Pine, sliding into a right hand turn at about forty miles per hour. Leaving a good amount of Goodyear rubber on the residential pavement, Officer Banks quickly straightened his steering wheel, darting down Shelby Street towards Hayes. Then, they saw them. Almost mid-block, there they were.

"Nine-Two pulling up, Radio. We do have one down. We're gonna check her right now and let you know," Banks notified dispatch.

As they exited the scout car, they both observed a motionless female lying across a curb with only her feet stretched out into the street.

"Nine-Two, Radio. Could we get an ETA on the EMS?" Banks asked Dispatch as she and Harper approached the scene on foot.

"Back up everybody, step back," Officer Harper ordered a woman who was in tears, crying uncontrollably as she sat on the grass next to the unconscious woman rocking back and forth.

"Ten minutes out, Nine-Two." Dispatch responded.

"Sir, move away," Banks repeated to an older man who was knelt down, also over the still body, appearing to search for her pulse.

"She's still alive," the older man shouted.

Realizing that the two upset individuals that were at the scene were intoxicated, Officer Harper helped the distraught woman to her feet as Banks knelt down to check for any signs of life.

Partially lying on her side, Officer Banks rolled the victim onto her back. "What happened?" he asked, noticing a very small amount of blood smeared half way down the left side of her face.

"We don't know," the older man answered aggressively.

With such an extensive career that exposed Banks to experiences that included a multitude of scenes where death was involved, she could tell at first glance that the unconscious female was more than likely, already deceased, but with the lack of blood at the scene, she had to verify. If even just for the slightest hint of life.

"She was just breathing a second ago," the older man repeated.

Ignoring him, Officer Banks placed her fingers on the victim's neck to check her breathing. Almost immediately, she realized that she was unfortunately correct. The unknown woman was in fact, deceased. Still kneeling, Banks looked back over her shoulder at her partner and shakes her head. Without saying a word, the nod and the expression on her face let Harper know that the unresponsive woman was already gone.

"Nine-Two, Radio could you send us a supervisor to our location," Harper requested.

"What? What's that look on your face mean?" the intoxicated woman questioned with overflowing emotions. "She ain't dead. She was just breathing," she continued in disbelief.

Holding the distraught woman back, Harper attempts to calm her down and extract any kind of information from her and her male acquaintance.

As Officer Banks and Harper made sure that the two individuals that they found standing over the deceased woman were unarmed, the other responding units arrived and helped to tape off and secure the scene.

With the inability to cover-up the deceased woman's body that remained lying in public view, along with a crowd of spectators, family and friends from the neighborhood gathering as everyone waited for the EMS to arrive, Harper made a quick and clever decision. He walked back up to the body, knelt down, and began to administer CPR.

"Harper, what are you doing? She's dead. I just checked," Banks asked.

"Listen," Harper told his partner as he repeatedly pushes down on the woman's already cold chest.

Off into the distance, just on the other side of the additional officers and police scene tape, Banks could hear the faint voices of the few rowdy persons mixed within the crowd yelling, "Why ain't they doin' nothin'? Why are they all just standing around? Call an ambulance. We don't need y'all. We need the ambulance."

Realizing the destructive potential behind the poisonous ranting that was sporadically being spewed out from within the fabric of the growing crowd, Officer Banks immediately understood the reasoning behind Harper's decision to create a perceptive illusion of being engaged in some kind of effective activity. "Radio, we're gonna need a couple more units over here for crowd control," she requested.

Shortly after, the ambulance arrived to the scene, bringing a much needed element to Harper's strategic ruse. The medics made the official confirmation of death and were able to cover-up the victims' body.

"How did she die?" Banks asked the EMT's. "She had some blood on her cheek, but I didn't see any wounds."

One of the EMT's kneeled back down, pulls the sheet covering the victim back and pointed to the left side of her head. "It was hard for us to find too," he says. "She was shot here, with a small caliber bullet. It was hidden by her hair in her scalp on the left side here."

Officer Banks took a look as the EMT pulled the deceased hair back. "Wow, there's hardly any blood. It must've been a twenty-two," she deduced.

"More than likely," the EMT replied.

"Hey guys, if you can, could you stick around for about five more minutes? I want this crowd to think that we're doing everything possible over here even though there's nothing else we can do for her," Harper asked.

"No problem. We'll stick around for a minute. We have to catch up some paperwork anyway," they replied.

As they awaited the arrival of their supervisor. Banks, Harper and the other units at the scene began to canvass the area, asking onlookers that knew the victim and nearby neighbors investigative questions in search for a history of the deceased and or any information on a possible perpetrator.

Through the heavy slurred speech and the incoherently disjointed dialog, Officer Harper eventually figured out that the drunken woman who was seated next to the victim when they first arrived to the scene was in-fact the victim's mother. She told him that her daughter's name was Kimberly Pierce and that she last saw her about three hours ago. Unfortunately, the mother went on to say that she had been drinking at a nearby home with her male companion that was also at the scene and didn't see what happened. She said that she only heard a gunshot and when she looked out of the front door, she saw her daughter two houses down, lying across the curb, with her legs stretched out into the street.

Officer Harper played out the horrible crime in his mind, attempting to figure out what happened and where the person who committed this crime could have fled.

With only about four homes on the block, going from house to house questioning the residents seemed to be a simple task. Seemed to be. Three of the homes were on the same side of the street as where the victim lay. The forth home was a neatly groomed little white house that stood alone on the opposite side of the street, directly across from the incident.

The first home was occupied by the victim's mother who was there inside, again, drinking at the time of the incident. The residents of the other two homes that were located on that same side of the street, were also inside of the home with the intoxicated mother, also drinking and the forth home, which was that one that stood alone was occupied by an eighty-five year old woman who stated that she was watching her shows on television and hadn't heard a thing.

As the back-up units stood-by for assistance with crowd control they were approached and advised by several people claiming that they were the victim's family members and friends. They told the officers that the person who they thought murdered Kimberly was her abusive off and on boyfriend, Jamil Brewer. They gave a description of a muscular black male, about six-two, two hundred and forty pounds with shoulder length braided hair and glasses.

After being given a few more details, someone from in the crowd stepped forward and decided to share a very important piece of the puzzle. They stated that just before the police arrived, they observed Jamil Brewer walk into the lonely white house across from the active scene, where he lived with his grandmother.

Nine-Two was immediately notified, but by now the sun had completely gone down and visibility was proving to become a potential issue.

Officers from other units surrounded the house as Officers Banks and Harper cautiously walk up to the front door and knock. Again, it was answered by the eighty-five year old woman.

"Hello, ma'am. It's us again," Harper said with a calming smile.

"Oh, hello there. I'm sorry it took so long for me to get to the door. I was watching my show," the elderly woman told them.

"I know. We apologize for the interruption. but we had a couple more questions. Is your grandson, Jamil, here?" Officer Banks asked.

"Yes he is. He's upstairs in his room," she replied.

"Great. Is it ok if we come in and talk to him for a minute," Banks asked her, using her charm.

"Sure, come on in," she told them as she unlocked the screen door.

But just as they walk in, a male matching the description of the wanted Jamil Brewer casually walked out of the kitchen and into the living room, towards them, but now he was bald.

Without an introduction, or even a single question asked, Mr. Brewer voluntarily exclaimed, "What did my brother do now? This man is gonna get me in trouble, again. I heard he was out there shooting with somebody earlier. If he thinks that I'm going back in for something he did, then he must be outta his mind. I did my time."

It was at that moment that Officers Harper and Banks instinctively determined that this conversation would probably be best continued in a more, controlled, secure manner.

"Mr. Brewer, correct?" Harper inquired.

"Yeah, that's me," he answered.

Both officers cautiously walked towards Brewer, approaching him from either side, "Ok, sir. For your safety and ours, we're gonna need to place these cuffs on you right quick. Just so we can figure out what's going on," Officer Banks explained, again, using the charming calm in her voice.

As Harper grabbed the wrist of Brewer, Brewer's first instinct was to resist.

"We appreciate your patience in cooperating with us. We just didn't want any kind of mistakes to happen with your grandmother here. We gotta keep her safe, you know, you now?", Harper suggested, attempting to distract and calm Mr. Brewer from any thought of further resistance.

"I get it. Y'all just doin' your jobs," Brewer replied as he decided to cooperate, placing his hands behind his back to be handcuffed.

"Oh, Jamil. Y'all officers not takin' him to jail, are you?" the grandmother asked.

"We're just talking right now ma'am. We have to get an understanding about what happened outside earlier today," Officer Banks explained.

Meanwhile, as Officer Harper checked the surroundings of the couch and seats including the cushions, he noticed dozens of live twenty-two caliber rounds lying on the floor, scattered throughout the room that led to a small paper bag that was half full of more live rounds. With no weapon found, he made a decision to make his and his partners' surroundings even safer and even more in their command. "You guys can have a seat while we figure this out and wait for our supervisor," he suggested.

As they wait, Officer Banks asked, "Is there anybody else here?"

The grandmother answered no, but Mr. Brewer replied, "Nah, my brother is gone. That's the one y'all lookin' for."

"What do you mean that's who we are looking for?" Harper asked.

"I ain't done nothin'. I've been asleep all day. This is my first time down stairs today," Mr. Brewer replied.

"Well where is your brother? And what's his name?" Harper questioned.

"His name is Jamil and I don't know where he's at," Brewer responded.

Puzzled, Banks asked, "Jamil? If he's Jamil, then who are you?"

"My name is Jamal. Jamil is my twin brother."

Stunned and completely taken off guard, Harper and Banks remain skeptical and find his twin brother story hard to swallow.

"So you're not Jamil, and you didn't just cut your braids off earlier today?" Harper asked.

Brewer chuckles and denied Harper's insinuation. "No sir. We look just alike, only he wears glasses. That's one reason why I cut my braids off when I got out of prison. He was too hot. He had too many people after him."

"Okay, so when was the last time you saw your brother?" Banks asked.

"I haven't seen him all day," he answered.

"What about you, ma'am?" Officer Harper asked the grandmother.

"Ain't that him right there?" she asked, pointing at Brewer.

"Grandma! It's me, Jamal! Remember? Jamil has braids and wears glasses!" Brewer claimed in response to his grandmother's reply.

"Hey, hey now, don't yell at your grandmother. Banks told Brewer.

"Nah nah, officer. She can't hear or see that well. You gotta shout at her," Brewer responded.

Harper smiles, "She just called you Jamil, Jamal. What now?" he says sarcastically.

"Man," he paused. "Officer, my I.D. is upstairs in my room. Please go get it. I am not my brother," Brewer pleaded.

"Your I.D.? Or your brother's I.D.?" Harper skeptically asked.

"Mine, sir. My I.D. is right upstairs in my room. You can go get it right now, Sir," Brewer replied.

"So you're saying that it's ok for us to go upstairs and look for your I.D.?" Harper asked, attempting to clarify his permission to search upstairs.

"If that's the only way y'all gonna believe me, go ahead," Brewer replied.

Their supervisor eventually arrived with another pair of officers. They checked the upstairs bedroom for Mr. Brewers I.D. where they found, not only identification that read Jamil Brewer, but clippings of shaved hair and a loaded twenty-two caliber rifle.

While waiting to complete the search, Brewers grandmother continued to refer to Brewer as Jamil. Taking her age and mental health under consideration, Banks and Harper's supervisor decide to officially place Brewer into custody and transported him to processing where the homicide unit could investigate further.

"Alright, Mr. Brewer. Per our supervisor, we're gonna have to take you downtown to figure all this out. We want to make sure you're ruled out and you don't get blamed for something your brother did. Sounds good?" Banks explained in her calming tone.

"Okay, but could y'all lockup so my grandmother will be safe for the night?" Brewer requested.

"Of course. We got her. No problem," Banks assured him.

"Thank you. One more thing, I didn't take my medication today. Can I take it before I go?" he asked.

"We can't give you any medication, but we can take it with us and they can refill your script and give it to you where you're going." Officer Harper explained.

"Thank you. It's over there on top of the refrigerator," Brewer replied.

Harper walks over to the refrigerator to get the bottle of pills and noticed a pair of glasses sitting next to it.

"Do you want your glasses too?" Harper asked.

"Nah, those are my brothers," he answered.

Harper walked the bottle of medicine over to Brewer and asked, "Is this it?"

Inches from Brewer's face, he replied, "I'm not sure. I can't see it. Can I use my brother's glasses right quick?"

"I thought you said that you didn't wear glasses," Banks asked.

"Nah nah. His glasses ain't as strong as mine."

"You sure, Jamal?" Harper inquired with sarcasm.

Brewer smiled. "Yeah man. They're not mine," he replied.

Officer Harper placed the glasses on his face and said, "I don't see how you're gonna be able to read anything if the script to your lenses are stronger, but here you go."

With no squinting, he easily read the label on the bottle. "Yeah, that's it. Thank you, Officer."

Banks laughed as Harper hands her the glasses to give to his grandmother.

"Umm. I might need those later," Brewer says before he walks out the door.

"You know what? Here Jamil. Just take your stuff so we can go," Banks exclaimed, fed up with Brewer's games.

"It's Jamal, Officer," Brewer replied.

"Yeah, Okay Jamil. We got it." Banks replied to him.

Harper and Banks finally transported Brewer for processing and to speak to a homicide detective where after two days, he was released. After further investigation, the actual Jamil Brewer, identical twin brother to Jamal Brewer, was eventually located and arrested for murder. He told the investigators that he cut all of his braids off and stole his brothers' I.D. before he left that night so he could try to cross over into Canada, undetected. Fortunately, he was caught just in time.

- C O N C L U S I O N -

A possible blessing, or a curse? In all law enforcement entities, the investigating officer or agent has an undesired obligation to remain skeptic to all statements, and enter the mindset of the criminal and try to think, essentially, as the criminal would think. As if they were the thief, the drug dealer, or the murderer. An effective and necessary tool in most situations.

This method must be used when conducting an investigation as an officer in order to successfully solve crimes. Although this form of psychoanalysis, can become a type of black hole gateway to a kind of, self-inflicted, mental abuse that spawns the potential to destroy its own creator if left unchecked.

CHAPTER / twelve

Finding Mr. Foster

Over the tenure of an officers' career, the amount of exposure authored by the madness of men can often prove to be unsettling on an intimate basis. Officers are constant first hand witnesses to the limitless atrocities that occur daily. Sometimes, personal beliefs and ethics get in the way of professionalism and have to be put on standby in the best interest of certain cases in order to successfully apprehend and convict, what most consider to be, one of the most heinous kind of criminals in existence.

-CASE HISTORY-

Officer Kendal Gardner was the epitome of a family man. He would always start his mornings off with dropping his fraternal twins, a boy and a girl, off to their middle school, located only a half of a mile away from home. See, working as an officer for the past eleven years, gave him a certain insight on Murphys law, and when it came to his children, Gardner made sure that he maintained as much control as he could, with the billions of chance possibilities that could happen.

With his wife working days and his kids in school, Kendal took his weekday morning hours and used them wisely. Each day, he would complete a task after dropping his children off and then immediately get some rest before returning back to work for the afternoon shift. Knowing that his wife would pick their kids up from school, Kendal was able to depend on the routine daily. Unable to see his family before he left the house, Gardner would religiously call his wife to check up on her and the twins on the way into work, as well as while he was at work.

On this day, Officer Gardner would go to work, only to find out that he would be patrolling alone. While attending roll call, he found out that his partner had called in, making the man power count for two-man units uneven. Now working as one-man Adam unit, Gardner knew that he had to report back to the precinct by nightfall for safety reasons. With a full staff of personnel working inside the precinct, Gardner decided to request to use some of his time to slide out for the remainder of the day, hoping that he could maybe spend some time with his family and possibly tuck his kids into bed. But the rigger of the job is demanding and sometimes it beckons with a conviction.

It was late September and the sun started to fade around seven-thirty in the evening. Officer Kendal Gardner was assigned to work patrol unit Forty-Two Adam-One. With all of the other patrol units busy on high priority runs and only plain clothed officers possibly available, dispatch decided to give Gardner, who was in uniform, one more run before he had to report back to the station.

Dispatch assigned Gardner a police run. "Forty-Two Adam-One, Forty-Two Adam-One, make 23744 Peer Street on family trouble, possible child abuse. Mother says that she just returned home from work and her four year old daughter has a bruise on her shoulder and is complaining of stomach pain. She added that the baby-sitter is still there waiting for the police. EMS is requested."

"Show Forty-Two Adam-One on the way, Radio," Gardner acknowledged.

With only a sliver of day light remaining, Sergeant Miller of the precinct's plain clothes unit also acknowledged Officer Gardner's police run, "Radio, this is Forty-Nine Sam. Show me making that location with Forty-Two Adam-One. I'm about ten minutes out," he told dispatch.

"Forty-Nine Sam, I show you headed that way," Dispatch replied.

With several kinds of incentives running through Gardner's head, he hurries to the police run hoping that the child in question was fine and that the mother was just a very over dramatic parent. But when he arrives to the run, he finds that the situation is all but too real.

Gardner notified dispatch that he was at the scene as he walked up to the front door and knocked, "Hello? Someone call the police?" he queried, announcing his arrival.

"I show you at scene, Forty-Two Adam-One," dispatch acknowledged.

A teenager came to the door, "Hello," she said as she opened it. "You can come in."

"You guys call?" Gardner asked.

"Yes, Ms. Foster is in the back with Emily. You can follow me," the young lady told Gardner as she guided him to the four year old's bedroom in the rear of the home.

Just then, Sergeant Miller arrived to the location. "Dispatch, show Forty-Nine Sam at scene," he notified the dispatcher.

Meanwhile, Officer Gardner is just entering the bedroom where the mother and daughter were waiting. Crying and in obvious discomfort, Emily, the four year old, lay curled up in a tight ball clutching her stomach under the covers of her bed as her mother, Ms. Foster, desperately tried to console her.

"Mommy, it hurts," she cried out, over and over.

Trying her best, Ms. Foster comforted her daughter, reassuring her that everything was going to be alright. She immediately turned her attention to Officer Gardner as he walked into the room. "Where's the ambulance? We don't need you. We need an ambulance, she has to go to the hospital!" she told Gardner.

"Yes ma'am, they're on their way. But you must've mentioned to the operator that there was some kind of visible bruising on her also. So they sent me too," Gardner explained.

"Yeah, she has a little bruising on her upper arm, but she's having a lot of pain in her stomach right now. We need to go to the hospital. We can figure this other stuff out later," she replied to Gardner.

"Okay, that's fine. They're coming. In the meantime, can I ask you some questions? I just need a little information," Gardner asked.

Just then, Sergeant Miller walked into the room and introduced himself, "Hello. I'm Sergeant Miller."

"Hi," Ms. Foster answered. She then agrees to answer the officers' questions as she asked the babysitter, who was still there, to take over comforting little Emily.

After asking the pertinent contact information questions, Officer Gardner asked Ms. Foster about the child's father, "Is the father in the picture?"

"No. He died a few years ago. It's just my daughter and me," she responded.

"Did you see this bruise on her before you left for work?" Gardner followed up in his questioning.

"Look, you're worried about the wrong thing right now. My baby needs to go to the hospital," Ms. Foster urged with building frustration.

"Ma'am, they should be here soon, but I'll go check on that right now for you," Sgt. Miller reassured her.

Ms. Foster returned to her daughter who continued writhing in pain, "Baby, they're coming. It's just gonna be a little bit longer," Ms. Foster told her daughter. "Do you want something?" she asked Emily. "Your bear? Some ice chips?"

"No," Emily replied to her mother. "I think that I have to use the bathroom."

"Okay baby. Come on. I'll help you," her mother replied.

As Emily and her mother go to the restroom, Officer Gardner pulled the teen babysitter aside to ask her additional questions, "What's your name?" Gardner asked.

"Brianne," she answered.

"Are you the only babysitter for Emily?"

"That I know of, yes."

"Is this the first time that you've seen that bruise on Emily's arm?"

"Yeah, I didn't even know she had that until her mother asked me about it when she got home."

"And you have no idea of how it got there?"

"No I don't, and I didn't do anything to hurt her either. In case that's what you're trying to get at!" Brianne told Officer Gardner with a defensive attitude.

"Okay. I just need to ask these questions for clarification. It's all in Emily's best interest. You understand, don't you?" Gardner replied.

"I get it. I do, but I want to let y'all know that there's no way that me or Ms. Foster would do anything to hurt Emily," she explained.

"Okay, good, good," Gardner responded, continuing with his questions.

"EMS is here," Sergeant Miller shouted from the front door.

"Thanks Sarge," Gardner replied. "Could you let Ms. Foster and Emily know that the Ambulance has arrived?" he asked Brianne.

"Sure, one second," she said as she walked to the bathroom door. "Ms. Foster, the ambulance is here."

Sergeant Miller walked up to Gardner and got a quick briefing on the visible injury on Emily's arm.

"The babysitter and the mother say they have no idea how that bruise got on the little girl's arm," Officer Gardner told Sergeant Miller.

"Oh really?" Miller asked sarcastically. "Well what did they feed her? I mean she's really doubled over there."

"I don't know. Whatever it is, hopefully she got it out in the bathroom," Gardner answered.

"Well find that out and write up an informational report just in case, you know? That bruise came from somewhere. Either by playing or by some other means, but it's a visible injury and you best cover your backside," Miller advised Gardner.

"Roger that, Sarge," Gardner replied. "Brianne, I have a couple more questions for you while the medics look over Emily."

Brianne agreed as she gathered her things, preparing to go home.

"We're curious, what did Emily eat that could of possibly made her stomach hurt so bad?" Gardner asked.

"I'm not sure. She only had some apple sauce while I was here. She was fine before I left," Brianne answered.

At a lost, Gardner questioned, "What do you mean, before you left?"

"She mentioned that her stomach started hurting when I got back. I told her to just lay down if she didn't have to use the bathroom," Brianne explained.

"You went somewhere while you were supposed to be here watching her?" he asked.

"Just for a minute, but, Peter was here."

"Who is Peter?"

"That's her uncle, her dad's brother," she answered.

204 | P a g e

It was at that moment that the mentality of an officer kicked in. Sergeant Miller and Gardner look at each other.

"Tell the medics to hold up," Miller instructed Gardner.

"Fellas, I need you to hold on for me right quick," Gardner said to the EMS crew.

"How long was he here alone with Emily?" Miller asked Brianne.

"Just about thirty to forty-five minutes," she answered.

"And he left when you got back?" he continued.

"Yes. He seemed a little out of it too."

"What do you mean, a little out of it?"

"Like he was high or something."

"And he didn't say anything to you?" Miller asked.

"Not really," she replied. "He just left."

"Okay. You hold tight for me. We may need some more information from you," Miller requested.

"That's fine. I have time," Brianne agreed.

Miller walked up to Ms. Foster and discretely asked, "Ma'am. My apologies for holding you up. I just have a quick question for you. Is that okay?"

Still worried and upset, she answered, "Yes Officer, but please can we hurry?"

"Absolutely," he replied. "When you took your daughter to the bathroom, did you notice anything?"

"What do you mean?"

"Did she actually use it? Did anything come out? Did she say anything to you?" Miller asked

Confused with the type of questions, Ms. Foster said, "No...she didn't say anything to me. She was just in a lot of pain so I told her to just get off of the toilet when the ambulance got here."

"And she didn't actually use it, did she?" Miller questioned further as Gardner overheard and then joined the conversation.

"No. I don't think so," she answered.

"Ms. Foster, do you have a brother-in-law named, Peter?" Miller inquired.

Hesitantly, she answered, "Yes, why?"

Realizing that Miller's questioning was leading down a one-way street, Gardner asked, "Ms. Foster, did you happen to examine your daughter's underwear?"

"What do you mean, examine her underwear?" she asked with a build of disgust.

"Ms. Foster, we have to exclude any idea of a possible criminal act. So we're asking if you can help us out and just take a look to see if you see anything, like spots of blood, or anything that might raise a red flag," Miller explained.

Extremely outraged at the idea, Ms. Foster decided to go ahead and examine Emily's underwear. "Emily, baby come to mommy," she told her daughter. "Mommy just wants to make sure you have on some clean undies before we go see the doctor, okay? You know what mommy always says; we always want to be clean, right?"

"Yes Mommy," Emily agreed.

Ms. Foster pulled Emily back into the bathroom and checked her daughter's toddler sized underwear and discovered that there was no blood at all.

"No officer," Ms. Foster said with an impatient attitude as she exited the restroom. "She's perfectly fine. Can we go now?"

"Great, thank you," Miller replied. "Yes, you guys can go get little Emily all better now.

"See, Mommy. I put my dirty panties in the dirty clothes. I stay clean just like you always tell me. I'mma big girl."

This was the point where everybody that was in that room at the time experienced a kind of cardiac event.

"Emily...baby-girl. Honey, what do you mean? Did you change your undies today already?" her mom nervously asked.

Still holding her stomach, Emily smiled with a since of accomplishment and nodded, yes. "Emmhmm...and I wiped myself too."

In total shock, her mother began tearing up. "Baby, what are you saying? What did you have to wipe?

"Umm, Emily," Miller interrupted. "You're such a good big girl. You and mommy can head on up to the hospital and let the doctor take a look at you, okay?"

"Okay, Mr. Policeman," Emily replied.

"One thing before you go, Em. Can I call you Em?" Miller asked Emily.

"Sure."

"I wanna help you and mommy stay clean, okay? Can you point out where you put your dirty clothes so I can get them all cleaned for you ?"

Emily looked at her mother. Beginning to understand the impossible, Ms. Foster gives Emily the okay. "Go ahead, baby. You can tell him."

Emily pointed and said, "I put them over there," Directing them to a chair in her room.

"They're over there?" Gardner asked.

"Emmhmm," she replied. "At the bottom."

"Why did you put them there, Emily?" her mother asked.

"I was scared."

"Scared of what, baby?" she inquired.

"It was supposed to be a secret," Emily explained.

"Okay, Ms. Foster. You can take Emily to the hospital now. We'll take it from here. You just be there for your daughter," Sergeant Miller told her.

Ms. Foster hugged Emily tightly as they headed to the ambulance.

With a sickness building in his stomach, a lump forming in his throat, Officer Garner walked over to the chair Emily pointed at and with all of the professionalism that he could muster, he peeked under the chair and observed something white tucked away, deeply underneath. He took in a deep breath and exhaled in an effort to help him prepare for what his experience screamed at him. Firmly gripping either arm of the chair, he lifted it and moved it out of his way and there they were.

Gardner knelt down, and without touching it, he took his pen and opened them, uncovering the sickness of man. Lined throughout the inside of Emily's underwear was an excessive amount of human discharge, mixed with grotesque stains of blood.

With a foul nausea stirring in his stomach, Officer Gardner and his sense of family and principles of human decency transformed his mind into pure rage.

"Sarge!" Gardner shouted.

"Whatchu got?" Miller responded.

"Green light. The evidence is confirmed. You better get him before I do!"

"Calm down now. I'm gonna send my crew to find him and you better believe he'll be in cuffs by the end of the shift. You just process the scene, make your notifications and make your report.

Child Abuse and Special Victims will conduct the victims' statement."

"Copy that, Sarge. You guys let me know when you got him."

"I'll call you when we do."

A couple of hours went by as Gardner processed the scene and there was no word from Sergeant Miller or his plain clothes unit. Friends and neighbors stop by to see what was going on and pretty much every specialized unit that was supposed to make the scene had also already came by and conducted their part of the investigation. Gardner was just sitting in his scout car writing his report when something completely unexpected happened, Uncle Pete decided to drop by.

Obviously intoxicated, Uncle Pete staggered up the front porch stairs, desperately clinging to the rail in order to prevent an eventful tumble backwards.

Gardner picked up his walkie and radioed in to Dispatch, "Yeah, umm. Can you let Forty-Nine Sam and his crew know that I found our perp. He's kindly decided to join us in the search for himself."

"Is he at the scene with you, Forty-Two Adam-One?" Dispatch asked.

"That's an affirmative, Radio."

"Forty-Nine Sam. Cars in District Forty. Forty-Two Adam-One has a perp that has returned to the scene at 23477 Peer Street," Dispatch announced.

Knowing Gardner's mindset, Sergeant Miller hustled to the scene. "Forty-Nine Sam ninety seconds out," Miller acknowledged. "Tell that unit to stand by for backup if he can."

Before dispatch could relay the message, Gardner responded, "Yeah, Radio. Let that unit know that I won't be able to wait. He's walking over to me as we speak."

But the truth was, Pete was still intoxicated and could barely walk. He also hadn't a clue that any officer was there. That's when Miller knew he had to get there, not for Officer Gardner's safety, but for the sake of Uncle Pete's safety.

Officer Gardner exited his scout car and calmly approached his perpetrator. "Hey, Pete. What's up, man? How's it hanging?" he shouted as he tightened his leather gloves.

"Who is that? Who are you? You don't know me," Peter slurred uncontrollably.

Gardner got to the foot of the porch stairs. "Hey, buddy. Why don't you come here right quick so I can ask you something?" he coaxed him.

Completely out of it, Pete made his way from the door down to the second of the four steps. Completely fueled with a focused rage, Gardner reached out to Peter with intentions of a rough introduction.

Gardner grabbed him by his coat. He gripped tightly, then, Sergeant Miller touched his shoulder.

"Kendal," he exclaimed. "You have too much to lose, Bro. I got this. You can go."

Still furious, but now in control, Gardner snapped out of his ill-advised mindset and thanked Miller, "Thank you, Sarge. You saved me and you kept your word. He looks good in your cuffs."

Peter Foster was then taken down to the district and charged with several felonies including the rape of a minor. He stated to investigators that he didn't remember anything that he did that day and that he had been constantly on a bender and high for days up until his arrest. The evidence collected matched Mr. Foster's DNA and was vital in his conviction.
Emily eventually got better, emotionally, physically, and mentally. While in her late teens now, Emily holds her head high and still refuses to give Uncle Pete anymore of the time in her life.

- C O N C L U S I O N -

With this horrific case, the officer found himself at a crossroad. Blinded by his rage and nearly crossing the line, this officer and the core of his principles were heavily tested. It's moments like these that professional responsibility become paramount. With a blind will to condemn, multiplied by the idea of a tragedy that can just as easily become one's own at any given time, personal beliefs can quickly distort ethics and drive him or her down a dark misguided path. Focused vision with blinders can easily mirror a reckless and opposite desired effect. It's an art form to just possess the skill of recognizing this type of handicap and make adjustments accordingly, placing those deeply rooted morals and ritualistic practices and principles on standby in the best interest of the case at hand, in an effort to apprehend and convict successfully... And it doesn't hurt to have someone that you can rely on to support you and have your back also.

CHAPTER / thirteen

The Shoe Actually Does Fit

There comes a time in everyone's life where a person realizes that there are limits to what they are capable of. Not many occupations can attest to the frequency of this fact as much as law enforcement. Doctors perform textbook procedures on their patients, lawyers master and manipulate the law in an effort to control the individual minds of twelve jurors, and police officers can only investigate as far as the evidence takes them. It's at that point where things like creativity, miracles and just plain old luck decides to step in, tipping the scales and triggering progress.

-CASE HISTORY-

Officers Christopher Hart and Joseph Daniels, working school unit Charlie-One-Eighty-One reported into work a couple of hours earlier than the regular patrol crews did because they were responsible for assisting with the children's commute to school in the mornings. Hart and Daniels routinely began their shift off with a strong cup of coffee and a quick survey of any pertinent and relatable criminal activities that had transpired from the day before, up to the most recent shift. In the past, there were reports of kids being accosted, approached, followed and in some cases, attempted abductions and worse. So Officers Daniels and Hart took their assignment personal and made sure that they went above and beyond, daily.

The start of this day was no different from any other. After retrieving their gear, daily intelligence on criminal activity and a coffee, they would usually check the routes that the children traveled on the way to school. Checking alleyways, vacant homes and suspiciously parked vehicles.

Everything was routine...until it wasn't.

"Officer, officer!" an adult volunteer crossing guard shouted as she waved down Daniels and Hart's scout car. Surrounded by about a dozen children, she leaned over at Hart's passenger side window. "These two boys told me that there was a naked man in an alley about two blocks that way."

"Really?" Hart asked with disgust and disbelief.

"He was sleeping," one of the kids said.

"Sleep?" Hart replied. "You guys okay? He didn't hurt or try to touch any of you, did he?"

"No. He was sleepin' under his covers," the other kid told Hart. "It's white."

Uncertain what the boy meant, Daniels asked, "The man or the covers?"

"Nooooo. The cover is white with yellow flowers on it," the boy replied.

"The man was white too," the other boy added.

"Okay. Good, good. Which way did you guys say?" Officer Hart asked.

Seemingly all at once, they point and yell out, "Over there!"

"Got it. Thanks guys. We will definitely go check that strange man out; meanwhile you big brave kids go on ahead to school, and stay safe, okay?" Hart responded.

"Bye, Mr. Officer! Bye!" the kids shouted.

Hart and Daniels wave goodbye to the group of children and immediately head in the direction of where the kids pointed. They notified the dispatcher of what they were doing and where they were going. "Radio, this is Charlie-One-Eighty-One, copy?"

"Go ahead Charlie-One-Eighty-One," Dispatch answered.

"Yeah. Can you show me and my partner searching the area and alleyways in the vicinity of Pilgrim and Conner? We were flagged down by a crossing guard and a couple of school kids on a possible intoxicated white male sleeping in an alley over there. It's near the school, so we're gonna just check'em out right quick," Hart explained to the dispatcher.

"Copy that, Charlie-One-Eighty-One. I show you heading over there for an investigate person," Dispatch responded.

As they drove around checking the area that was pointed out to them, they had already made up their minds to wake the man up and transport him to a shelter, away from the surrounding schools nearby.

"Let's just get him up and out of here so that we can check the rest of our schools and then grab something to eat," Daniels suggested.

"I gotta agree with that. I'm starving," Hart replied.

With only three more alleys to check, Officer Daniels began to doubt the value of the two young boy's story. Was it a tale of children, or a tale of truths?

As options wound down, Hart and Daniels pull up to the next alley.

"Is that him right there?" Daniels asked.

With too much debris scattered throughout the alleyway, they parked the scout car at the mouth of the alley and got out in order to take a closer look.

"Yeah, that's him alright," Hart confirmed with contempt in his voice. "Sir! It's the police. Time to wake up and go!" he shouted.

"Umm, Chris..." Daniels said with a calm tone.

"I don't see why those kids came through this way to get to school anyway," Hart wondered as he and Daniels continued walking towards him.

"Uhhh...yeah, Chris buddy."

"Radio. We found him. Show us at Figaro and Jasper in the alley investigating one." Hart notified dispatch. "I mean, not only why would those kids cut through such a junky alley, but what kind of drugs would possess a person to fall asleep in all of this mess?" he continued with his fussing as he avoided the many average alleyway booby traps.

"Christopher," Daniels called out.

"Sir!!! You have to get up. You don't want me to have to come all the way over there; believe me." Hart warned.

"OFFICER!" Daniels shouted to his partner with desperation.

"What is it?" Hart finally replied as he picked his head up and looked over to his partner.

"I think he's gonna need you to go ahead on over to him," Daniels suggested.

"Why?" Hart asked as he looked over to the man lying in the alley. "Oh, I see."

"Yeah, I'm pretty sure he's not asleep right now," Daniels pointed out.

"Call it in and I'll take a closer look," Officer Hart suggested.

As Officer Hart began making all of the pertinent calls, Officer Daniels decided to look the scene over before making their report. What he discovered was a scene straight out of a horror film.

"So what's it look like over there?" Hart asked when they both got back into the scout car to make their reports and await the other investigative units.

"It was bad, man. The madness that went into that," Daniels replied. "Write this down, because I'm only gonna say this one time."

"It's that bad? Okay, go ahead. I'm ready," he answered.

"First off, that's not a white cover. It's a shower curtain that he's halfway wrapped in. When I peeled the curtain back to see his injuries, I noticed that he had about nineteen stab wounds everywhere on his upper torso. His hands were tied behind his back and it looked like they cut his throat so deep that his head was barely still attached to his body," Daniels explained.

"They really wanted him dead. With all those injuries, how come I didn't see any blood on that white curtain? Did last night's rain wash it away?" Hart wondered.

"That's the thing, there is no blood. Whoever did that, definitely did it somewhere else and then dumped him off over here," Daniels replied.

As Daniels and Hart remained at the scene while all of the various departments came and conducted their specific investigations, they completed their reports and were able to return back in-service detail just in time for the schools to let out for the day.

A week and a half had gone by and Officers Hart and Daniels were assigned to work One-Thirty-Two for overtime on the afternoon shift. They received a police run on a family trouble in progress.

"One-Thirty-Two, One-Thirty-Two. Make 1414 Brandon Street on a disturbance. Woman stated that her boyfriend won't leave. She says he's throwing things around the house and won't give her back the keys to her car. No weapons seen at this time. That's 1414 Brandon Street on a family trouble," Dispatch relayed to One-Thirty-Two.

"Show us on the way, Radio," Daniels responded.

Midway through their shift, Daniels and Hart had been experiencing a steady day. Police run after police run, unit One-Thirty-One's day was shaping up to be a full, but uneventful day. That is until they received the Brandon Street run.

"Radio, One-Thirty-One, show us at scene," Daniels notified the dispatcher.

"One-Thirty-One. I have you at scene. Let us know what's going on when you can," Dispatch requested.

As they pulled up to the run location, they observed a shoeless man attempting to crawl through a bottom floor window. Daniels and Hart quickly jumped out of their scout car, ran up to the suspicious man and carefully assisted him back out of the opened window. They handcuffed him and patted him down just in case he had any weapons.

"Can you please help us in understanding what exactly you thought you were doing, crawling in the window?" Hart questioned.

"I'm just trying to get back inside and go to sleep," he answered.

After Officer Daniels and Hart checked the man for weapons, they allowed him to have a seat on the front porch. They could hear a woman inside of the home shouting at the top of her lungs about what seemed like random thoughts.

As if he was in a contest, the man began to just rattle off back to back sentences. "Thank God you guys are here, Officers. I need you to please do somethin' with this girl. She's trippin', I mean she's totally bananas. Can I have a cigarette?"

"Okay sir. First, do you live here?" Officer Hart asked.

"Yes, I do. Me, my girlfriend and that evil little dog of hers," the man answered.

"Good, good. Now tell us what's going on so we can try to help," Hart responded.

"I just came home and she started throwing my things out here in the front yard," the man claimed.

"What's your name?" Hart asked him.

"My name is Mark."

"Mark, what?"

"Ward... Mark Ward."

"Mr. Ward, what's your girlfriend's name?" Daniels asked him.

"Kinsey Butler," Mark answered.

"Where is she at? Is that her inside yelling?" Daniels asked.

"Yeah that's her. I told y'all she's crazy," the man answered. "Y'all need to go talk to her or something. I'm not about to put up with her dumb stuff all night."

Officer Daniels announced himself and then walked inside as his partner and Mr. Ward remained outside. A powerful odor of bleach exploded in his face as he entered.

"Wow, I'm glad to see you guys maintain a high sense of cleanliness, but you need to open some more windows or something," Daniels suggested. "I'm about to pass out in here."

Hart stood Mr. Ward up to his feet. "Let's go inside and sort this out. There's no sense of telling the whole neighborhood your business," Hart explained to him.

"She's probably back there in the kitchen," Ward suggested.

"Ms. Butler. Did you still need us?" Officer Daniels asked as he and his partner walked Mr. Ward through the living room and down a long hallway toward the kitchen.

Ms. Butler explained to Officer Daniels how she was fed up with her live-in boyfriend's extra after hour proclivities. Along with many other additional complaints, Ms. Butler went on and on and on talking about how her boyfriend, Mr. Ward, wouldn't help out around the house and how he didn't take care of her like he used to, and that she ultimately wanted him gone.

"Y'all don't have to arrest him. I just want him gone," Butler requested.

Officers Daniels and Hart knew that they had no legal right to force, command, coerce, or ask either one of them to leave their home. But the officers didn't want to have to return back there for another police run. Possibly even for something worse.

"I'm not going anywhere except to sleep in my own bed, under my own covers, and that could be with, or without you, my dear," Ward responded to Kinsey. "I didn't do nothing to nobody. You want me to go, then you're gonna have to get them to arrest me, Honey Bear," he told her with contempt.

"Well if y'all can't get along and neither one of you won't voluntarily leave to preserve the peace, then guess what?" Officer Daniels mentioned as he called the district to have them run both of their names through the computer.

"And that must be the computer at the district Bookfacin' and Chatsnappin' me. Here we go," Daniels joked, keeping the calm and preparing Ward for what was ahead. "Mr. Ward, go ahead and head out to the car for me, please."

"There y'all go again with that BS. What's that computer over there lying on me about?" he asked as he reluctantly turned around to head back to the front door.

"It's simple. Just a traffic warrant. You can take care of that can't you?" Officer Hart asked.

"That ain't nothin'. I'll be back here in a couple of hours, babe. I'mma need you to have that bath water ready when I get back. And try to straighten up a little while you're at it," Ward sarcastically told his girlfriend.

As Officer Daniels locked the cuffs on Ward, Ms. Butler reverted to the textbook regretful girlfriend.

"Y'all don't have to take him to jail. See, y'all do too much. That's why nobody wants to even deal with y'all," Butler exclaimed as she began to tear up.

"Ma'am, you called us to handle your business and that's what we are doing," Daniels explained.

"See what you did? Now you wanna switch it up," Ward taunted.

"Nope. That's okay. I changed my mind," Butler pleaded.

"Ma'am, could you get your man's shoes so we can get going?" Hart asked.

"No, I'm not doin' nothin'. Y'all ain't gotta take him," Butler complained as she grabbed a piece of tissue to wipe the tears from her face.

"It's too late, Ms. Butler. The quicker we can leave, the quicker you can have him back. We just need his shoes, please." Daniels requested once more.

"I'm not getting nothin'. You want it; go and get it yourself!" she replied angrily.

"Fine Ms. Butler. Where are they?" Daniels asked.

Butler pointed to the basement stairwell. "There they go, right there," she directed him as she threw her tissue in the bathroom garbage while angrily walking to the front door.

Officer Hart grabbed Ward's arm. "Have a seat so you can put your shoes on," he told Ward as they walked back into the living room.

Officer Daniels walked to the stairwell and turned on the basement lights. Only a couple of steps down, Daniels stepped down onto the stairs, but the further he walked down the steps the more powerful the bleach odor became.

At a glance, Officer Daniels could tell that the overwhelming bleach smell was definitely coming from the basement. He could see an almost reddish-pink swirl pattern all over the basement floor. "Somebody cleaned the hell out of this basement. Did he help you with cleaning up down here?" Daniels asked sarcastically as he walked back to the living room.

But the walk back down that long hallway to the living room became a little more educational this second time around. What Daniels didn't notice on the first walkthrough was the decor. Because Ms. Butler left the bathroom door halfway opened when she threw her tissue away, Officer Daniels noticed a very peculiar detail. Stunned, and a mind being flooded with all kinds of thoughts, his interest peeked. As Daniels extended his arm out to hand Mr. Ward his shoes, he sees the confirmation to the thoughts that flooded his mind. Old brown blood stains that covered a third of the base of Ward's left shoe. The stain was smeared along the bottom side and sole of the shoe. And three small droplets screamed for attention seated at the top of the tongue.

He dropped the shoes to the floor. "EVERYBODY, FREEZE!" Officer Daniels shouted as he pulled his weapon.

"Awww, here we go Kinsey baby. They about to shoot us. Get the camera," Ward exclaimed.

"Joe," Officer Hart calmly called out with complete confusion.

"First y'all gone take my baby to jail for no reason, now y'all gone shoot us? Oh hell naw. Not today. Not me. You got me messed up if you think..."

"Kinsey!" Ward interrupted. "Baby, could you please shut the hell up before they kill us; me. I'm not trying to die today."

"Whateva." Butler replied.

"Gotchu," Daniels said with a smile. "Cuff her, Chris."

"My pleasure, partner. You wanna tell me what we're doing here?" Hart replied.

"Officer. Yo boy trippin'. How you just gonna go from completely calm with us, straight to pullin' guns out on us? I mean, do not pass go. Do not collect two hundred dollars type of crazy," Ward joked.

"You think you're funny, huh? You two have to be the dumbest criminals on the planet," Daniels replied.

After Hart placed Ms. Butler into cuffs, Daniels suggested, "Hey, partner. Check these nice shoes out."

Hart walked over and leaned over to take a closer look. "That's blood on your shoes Mr. Ward," Hart so studiously pointed out.

"Man, ain't no blood on my shoes. Both of y'all musta had a bad donut," Ward jested once again as he laughed.

"No, he's correct, partner," Daniels replied with an even bigger smile on his face. "Well, half correct at least. See, if you look real close, you'll notice that the right shoe is virtually spotless. But somebody got lazy and only took the time to clean one of the shoes."

Suddenly, Ward's cocky bravado decided to pack-up and leave. "Dammit, Kinsey!" Ward shouted.

"What's wrong, Mark? You don't look like you're having a good time anymore. And your girlfriend is real quiet all of a sudden. I guess she's starting to remember what else she neglected to take care of," Daniels continued.

"Man, I don't know what you're talking about, Officer," Ward claimed again.

"Go check out the bathroom for me partner," Daniels told Hart.

Officer Hart walked over to the bathroom door, pushed the door all the way open and, "Holy hell..." was the limit to his vocabulary at that specific point in time.

"Yep, she forgot to get rid of the second shower curtain. You know Mr. Ward, the one that matches the one that you guys left in the alley over on Figaro and Jasper?" Daniels asked rhetorically.

It was at that moment, Mark Ward knew he had to throw up.

Officers Hart and Daniels immediately made their notifications and had their supervisor and evidence technicians make the location to collect any and all additional evidence that pertained to the case. Meanwhile Mr. Ward and Ms. Butler were arrested and charged with first degree murder.

Further investigation revealed that Mr. Ward came home and caught his live-in girlfriend and the male victim in the act of having an affair. Mr.

Ward admitted that he was enraged and went to the kitchen, retrieved a large butcher knife and returned back to the bedroom where he put the knife to the victim's throat and threatened to kill him if he didn't go into the basement with him.

Mr. Ward further confessed that he and Ms. Butler then tied him to a chair seated on top of their shower curtain where Ms. Butler, who later confirmed the statement, stabbed him over and over. Barely alive, Mr. Ward and Ms. Butler decided to hang the male victim upside down by his ankles and then cut his throat open, forcing out all of the blood in his body, ultimately killing him.

-CONCLUSION-

In this case, you learn that as an officer, a seemingly simple police run can easily reveal an unexpected turn of events. With only so much information to have in a case where there is very little to go off of, sometimes that officer is forced to sit back and wait, hoping that the criminal makes a mistake in the future where it can lead back to their original crime. Even the cases that may seem to have no connection to one another, can sometimes affect a case that may have crossed your path. With your guard constantly up, a good officer has to pay attention to all of the details and make as many mental notes as possible just in case the puzzle pieces from two different puzzle boxes fit the same picture.

Kristopher W. Allen

CHAPTER / fourteen

The Sins of the Father

On the journey of becoming an effectively proficient police officer, the unforeseen consequences that derive from circumstances beyond your control, occur more often than one would expect. A burden forged by the nature of the job, officers must quickly learn that there are no set limits to the depths that a suspect is willing to go through in order to escape their momentary situation. Including a resolution that carries a lifetime of consequential repercussions.

-CASE HISTORY-

It was a beautiful Thursday afternoon in the first week of Spring. Officers Teddy Williams and James Ross were partnered together working scout Eight-One. As their day wound down to a close, dispatch needed them to make one more run before they headed back in to the precinct for off duty roll call.

"Eight-One, Eight-One. Make Clay and University for a school crossing from three o'clock until three-thirty. Eight-One, that's Clay and University for a school crossing from three o'clock until three-thirty."

Relieved that they could use the school crossing run to take them out for the day, they quickly responded, "Show Eight-One on the way, Radio."

Ross and Williams made it to their run and immediately set up for their crossing. As they activated their oscillating overhead lights, they parked the scout car off to the side. Officer Williams and Ross then took their post at the crossing intersection directing both foot and pedestrian traffic.

"When it starts to get heavy, let's double the lights and then the pedestrians," Ross suggested.

"Sounds like a plan, partner," Williams replied.

Hundreds of kids filed out as the bell sounded. Nearby was a high school and middle school. With only that one major intersection for all of the students to use, Ross and Williams quickly realized that this crossing wasn't going to be as simple as they thought. What they figured would probably take a good twenty minutes at the most, ended up taking the entire thirty.

They headed back over to their vehicle and stood there as they observed how the traffic handled the now semi-tamed flow.

"Man, that was a lot of kids, Bro," Williams exclaimed with a look of relief on his face.

"Musta been about a million and a half to the third power of people out there," Ross joked. "Let's give it another five minutes and then we can head in."

With a combination of children getting out of school and walking home, along with other citizens that headed out into traffic after a hard day's work, the three o'clock rush hour commute got pretty thick. It didn't help that earlier that day, the city's construction crew had just set up their equipment in preparation for road work to begin over the coming weekend.

Standing at the hood of their scout car, both, Ross and Williams agreed to give it a couple of extra light changes before they headed in.

"It looks good to me partner. How about you?" Ross asked.

"Yeah. I'm good," Williams responded with an eagerness to get back to the station.

Facing Ross, Williams took a step backwards onto the curb. "Do we have time to fill the tank up on the way?" he asked.

As Ross walked to the driver's side door, he turned his head and answered, "I don't think we..."

"JAY! WATCH OUT!" Williams shouted, warning Ross of the speeding oncoming car.

Officer Ross quickly leaped out of the way, jumping onto the hood of their scout car, "Holy hell!" Ross belted out.

"You okay?" Williams questioned with worry.

"Oh, he's mine!" he replied with purpose as he jumped down off of the hood, hurrying to put his police cruiser into drive and smash down on the accelerator.

"Priority, Radio!" Williams yelled into the mic.

"There he is," Ross mumbled.

"Unit with a priority, go ahead," Dispatch responded.

"That's Eight-One, Radio," Officer Williams responded. "Show us east bound on Clay from University, following a brown Chevy Impala, plate number one-two-one Adam Adam Charlie, occupied one time."

A monitoring supervisor came over the air, "Sam Eight-Seventy-Two. What's their reason for the pursuit?" she inquired.

Still trying to catch-up to the speeding Chevy, Officer Williams replied, "He almost hit my partner and we are currently going forty miles per hour in moderate traffic, still trying to catch-up.".

"Did you copy that Sam Eight-Seventy-Two?" Dispatch asked, making sure that a supervisor was monitoring the situation.

"He's turning south onto Douglass, and he's using his blinkers, Radio," Williams updated Dispatch.

"Sam Eight-Seventy-Two, copy that. Tell that unit to use caution and keep transmitting all updates. I'm on my way to the area."

"Copy that last, Radio. Traffic is getting thick. It looks like he's pulling over here at Douglass and Webb. Yep, show us on traffic at Douglass and Webb."

"Cars in district Eight...Eight-One has that brown Chevy Impala stopped at Douglass and Webb. Use caution Eight-One," Dispatch advised.

Ross pulled behind the Chevy and he and Williams patiently sit there, observing any and all movement that went on inside, just in case. After about thirty to forty-five long seconds the driver of the Chevy held his license out the window.

"Go ahead and put your car in park, and without stepping out, put your car keys on the roof of the car for me," Williams ordered him over the PA as Ross cracked open his door just in case he had to jump out in a hurry.

The man complied by putting his car in park and then placing the keys on the roof of his car as ordered.

"You ready?" Ross asked Williams anxiously.

"Hell yeah. Let's do it," Williams replied.

Both officers tactically exited their scout car and approached. With about two steps ahead of Ross, Williams was able to see through the passenger side windows, giving him a better view of the driver's hands sooner than Ross could.

"Let me see your hands!" Ross shouted to the driver.

With his mind programmed with worry of just looking for possible weapons, Williams could see that although he didn't observe any weapons, the man in the Chevy had his fists balled up and was reluctant to raise them in the air.

With tension and nervousness building in the air, Williams readied his weapon and shouted, "Put your damned hands up, or we're gonna have a problem."

But because of that sudden shouting, he'd now lost his tactical positioning. Unlike before, now the driver knew there were two of them and where he was standing.

The driver immediately turned his head and instantly snapped into a full on panic. Just before Ross could get to the driver's door, the man threw about a half of a dozen small plastic baggies of what looked like marijuana from his tightly balled up closed fist, out of the passenger side window. He then slammed a single key into the ignition, started the car, and peeled off.

Officer Ross quickly jumped backward, again, desperately trying to avoid from being hit.

"He's running on us again, Radio! He threw several baggies out the window and almost hit my partner again," Williams quickly transmitted over the air as they both sprinted back to the cruiser.

"Where's he headed, Eight-One?"Dispatch responded.

"He's continuing south on Douglass."

"What's your speed?"

Submerged in the deep-end of the panic pool, the reckless driver drives aimlessly in a perfectly confused circle.

"We're going about fifteen miles per hour, Radio. It's too much traffic out here. Now he's cutting through a parking lot headed east on Webb. He's stuck at a light behind traffic," Williams replied.

Forced to a complete stop and to make a hurried strategic decision, he continues his flight.

"Now he's cutting back through the parking lot again. Now he's headed north bound on Douglass toward the freeway," Williams continued to update.

Dispatch quickly relayed, "Available units in district Eight. Eight-One is following that brown Chevy wanted for felony assault of a police officer and he's on Douglass headed towards the I-Seventy-Three from Webb."

Then, he makes the decision that not only put an end to his inept attempt to flee, but it almost put an end to several innocent civilian lives as well, including one that Officers Ross and Williams didn't see coming.

"Yep, he's getting on the freeway, Radio," Williams updated the dispatcher.

The brown Chevy skidded as it took a sharp right turn, narrowly missing an oncoming car. He started down the on ramp.

"He can't go anywhere. It's bumper to bumper down there," Ross pointed out as he too made a right turn.

"Holy Shit!"Ross and Williams simultaneously exclaimed.

"Radio! Send an EMS and Fire to I-Seventy-Three, east bound at Douglass!" Williams requested with dire urgency.

"What do you have, Eight-One?" Dispatch asked.

"Looks like that brown Chevy went airborne and landed on top of another vehicle in the far lane on the freeway. We're trying to get down there now," Williams informed dispatch.

With the traffic backed up going up the on ramp, the man in the Chevy was unable to stop at the speed that he was going as he traveled down the ramp. So he decided to steer left, causing his vehicle to go airborne. Clearing the first two lanes, the brown Chevy landed on the roof of a Ford sedan, crushing the driver side and smashing into the divider, ultimately struggling to balance, teetering back and forth

Unable to drive any further down the on ramp because of the thick standstill traffic, Officer Ross and Officer Williams bailed out of their scout car and sprinted down the grassy embankment, urgently trying to get to whomever that was trapped inside of the two damaged vehicles. But just as they ran onto the freeway, Ross noticed that the driver of the brown Chevy had already gotten out of his vehicle and jumped over the divider into the west bound lanes.

"Help them, Teddy. He's running!" Ross yelled to Williams, pointing at the accident as he sprinted to apprehend the fleeing perpetrator.

Like a deadly game of double dutch, the subject cautiously made his way across the three lanes and halfway up the westbound embankment. With traffic at a halt on the east side and traffic slowing down on the west side, Officer Ross was also able to cross the three lanes safely. Struggling to race up the extremely slanted embankment, the suspect stopped and turned around just as he reached the ascending grassy apex.

Failing to process the reasoning into why the suspect stopped and just turned around, Ross pulled out his weapon and aimed in.

"Hands! Let me see your hands!" Ross commanded the fleeing suspect.

"I give up," he replied as he raised his hands.

"Turn around and get down, now!" Ross ordered him.

"Ok, ok. I'm sorry. I'm stupid. I didn't mean it. I'm sorry Officer. Please, sir," he pleaded as he began crying face down into the grass.

"Don't move!" Ross told him as he placed cuffs on his wrists. "I got him, Radio. He's in custody and we're headed back now."

"Just, please tell me is he okay? Is my boy okay?" the suspect questioned Ross with a blanket of remorse draped over his face.

"I don't know, man. You got me over here with you. You crashed onto the top of that car pretty good, Bro," Ross replied as he grabbed the man by his arm to escort him safely back across the freeway.

"No, no...my boy?" he repeated to Ross.

"You mean to tell me that you know the person in the car that you landed on top of?" Ross inquired as they start to cross back over to the other side.

"No, Joseph. My son. He's two. He's in his car seat in the back of my car."

In complete shock, Ross hurried the subject to the divider screaming at his partner who was helping to free the occupant of the bottom vehicle, "Teddy! Check the Chevy! Check the Chevy! There's a boy inside!" he shouted with a build of an anxious concern.

Williams quickly handed the injured driver to another officer and scrambled back over to the Chevy with hopes that the boy would be unharmed. Failing to hear any crying or yelling from any child, Williams carefully climbed up to the barely balanced wreck, and there he was. But his eyes were closed.

"Hey, buddy. Can you hear me?" Williams calmly asked him.

There was no response...

"His name is Joseph," Ross informed Williams.

With only one side of the car accessible, Williams gently opened the rear passenger door. Although Joseph was still strapped into the car seat, it apparently wasn't fastened to the back seat correctly.

He moves a large bag out of his way. "Dammit!" Williams exclaimed in frustration. "The car seat came a-loose. He's on the floor of the backseat, Jay. I think I can reach in and grab him without the car sliding down."

"Give it a shot, but be careful," Ross replied.

"Joe? Hey buddy. Can you hear me? I'm coming," Williams calmly attempted to communicate with the two year old.

Still, no response.

"How's it looking?" Ross asked with the build of anxious concern.

"Almost, there. Got him!" Ross blurted out with excitement.

Just as Officer Williams pulled the young child from the back of the car, he woke up, yawning.

"There you are. Hey buddy. You okay?" Williams asked, attempting to keep him calm.

Two medic units made it to the scene and evaluated and transported everyone to the hospital. The one innocent driver from the car that was crushed was examined and released with only minor injuries, while the two year old boy, Joseph, was taken to a nearby children hospital where he was given a good bill of health. Apparently, little Joseph slept through the whole thing.

Once the Chevy was put back on the ground, officer's inventoried the interior and discovered nine pounds of marijuana in a garbage bag that was next to the child's unsecured car seat. Turns out that the nine pounds of marijuana probably saved little Joseph's life. The cushioning from the packaged narcotics absorbed a lot of the tumbling that Joseph experienced while strapped to his unfastened car seat.

The father was charged with multiple felonies which included, felony assault of an officer with a motor vehicle, felony alluding, controlled substance violation and child abuse. Sentenced to serve many years in jail, he ultimately lost his rights to his two year old son, Joseph.

- C O N C L U S I O N -

This was a case where the unknown could have caused an inconceivable amount of pain and consequence. Although the officers had no idea that the fleeing suspect would put a child in such imminent danger, let alone his own son, it is a common factor in policing society that sometimes innocent citizens are put in danger too often. This is why you check your foreground and background before you discharge your weapon; why you must consider bystanders when you initiate a vehicle pursuit; and why, with every action taken, it is prudent to weigh the further danger being posed to other citizens that you have sworn to protect.

Because there is a statistically high percentage that you or another function of law enforcement will more than likely have a repeat encounter with that same subject at some point in the future, it may mean that at times, the best action to take, is to observe, take note, and strategically allow the perpetrator to escape...for now.

Kristopher W. Allen

CHAPTER / fifteen

An Annual Tradition

Holidays can be the roughest time of the year when dealing with society's troubles. The variety of probabilities that can get an officer into trouble, typically increase dramatically. Anytime a group of people gather to celebrate, the chances for the need of law enforcement intervention can become paramount, quickly.

Intoxication, conflicting personalities, old feuds and the level of disregard for the law become more likely, while the level of inhibition, common sense, and a decent tone of morality, become less likely.

-CASEHISTORY-

It was another cold and snowy day in the city. Most officers would decline to work on those last few wintery holidays of the year, but the lack of seniority and or the desire for an increased monetary compensation can easily become determining factors.

An admirable and well deserved practice for those chosen officers, is that it's also an unwritten custom in allowing them to head home a little early, or in the case of one particular holiday, every officer is ordered off of the streets and into the station for safety precaution purposes, if possible.

December is a month known for bringing joyful holidays that are mainly spent with family and friends. In particular, the holiday that triggers the safety precaution and commands the notability for ushering in the ending of one year and the beginning of another. That annually celebrated day that brings in the birth of a renewed year is also known to commonly be accompanied by a certain type of, "loaded," tradition.

Officers James Andrews and Damon Baker were out on patrol working scout Twelve-Two on the afternoon shift. Snow plows and salt trucks desperately tried clearing the roads throughout the day, making driving conditions somewhat tolerable. With some remaining unplowed streets that left about ten to twelve inches of thick wet snow on the ground, manipulating some roads proved to be difficult. Struggling throughout the day, Andrews desperately fought to keep the patrol car under control.

"So, you think maybe it snowed a little too much, today?" Baker joked sarcastically.

"Umm, uhh nope. This isn't anything. I've seen worse." Andrews replied as he turned a corner and comically slid into a curb right on cue.

Baker laughed, "Hmm hmm. Were you this bad of a driver when it was worse?"

"Shut up! You could've driven. Ya lazy bum. You just wanted me to struggle with this mess instead of you," Andrews complained.

"It's not a competition question. It was basically a confirmation inquiry, Drews. I just need to know if I have to make a phone call to my wife and kids. You should probably call a loved one too. Because the combination of your driving and this weather is building up to be a perfect formula for a prolonged hospital stay," Baker continued with his jesting.

"I tell you what, we're not chasing anybody today," Andrews insisted.

"I'd prefer you to chase a parking space until they clear all of these roads or until we get a police run. We don't need to get stuck out here today," Baker cleverly suggested.

"I have some paperwork to catch up on from yesterday anyway. Plus, this snow is constantly kissing the undercarriage of this car with these unplowed streets. Call dispatch and let them know that we'll be making the station to catch up on some work," Andrews replied.

Approaching the last two hours of the shift, Officer Baker contacted dispatch and explained how horrible the road conditions were, then he advised them that if they were needed, they would be departing from paperwork at the station.

It was conventional behavior for most citizens to stay indoors when heavy snow fell, but it wasn't a guaranteed practice. Those that were out and about, roaming the streets in bad weather on the eve of a holiday, were usually up to no good, running to an open store at the last minute or simply driving from party to party. Then, there are the ones that are doing all three.

Taking the current time under consideration, the dispatcher realized that the call board needed to be maintained as well as the task of maintaining the safety of the crews that were still out on patrol, answering runs. Twenty-three hundred hours rolled around, which meant that pretty soon, all of the street supervisors would be calling down to the dispatch unit, requesting that all of the crews that were still out on patrol, make a beeline back into the station. It was a traditional safety precaution used by numerous cities and towns. The popular practice is annually utilized for the sole purpose of lowering the risk to any officer of being intentionally or unintentionally targeted; or simply struck by any of the hundreds of stray bullets that are regularly discharged on and around the stroke of midnight on every December thirty-first.

The dispatcher issued officers Andrews and Baker an easy run from the board. "Twelve-Two, scout Twelve-Two. I need you to take this run for me. Make Forth and Main for a tan minivan driving recklessly. Check the area and let me know what you find. They're probably just having a hard time with the hazardous conditions out there."

A seemingly simple police run, Baker happily responded, "We're on our way, Radio. Show us in route from the station."

Although the snow had stopped falling, the damage was already done. Realizing that the dispatcher had just issued them their last run of the day, Andrews and Baker, both telephoned their families to let them know that they were fine and that they would be headed home soon to celebrate the incoming New Year together.

Officers Baker and Andrews headed out to the dispatched run and soon realize that there was positively nothing going on in the area. As usual for that time of year in that area, everything was quiet. Even so now with the added sound muffling from all of the thick snow fall.

"Dispatch, show Twelve-Two pulling up and checking the area," Baker transmitted, projecting the light from his flashlight down each of the surrounding alleyways as they passed by.

"Twelve-Two, I have you at your scene. Let me know what you find and make sure you clear over the air so that I can show you busy back at the station," the dispatcher advised.

"Twelve-Two copy, Radio," Baker replied.

"Do you see anything?" Andrews inquired.

"No sir, no I do not," he answered as his flashlight began to struggle.

"Kill that light. I left mine at the station and we might need yours later. Let's check around one more time. Just to make sure we don't get called back out here in this mess. I want to get outta here before the shooting starts," Andrews suggested.

"Ok, but just once more. My fire stick just ran out of juice anyway," Baker agreed.

Little did they know, that what was about to transpire, would relentlessly haunt them in their dreams for months to come and change both of their lives, forever.

They turned the corner...

"I still don't see anything," Andrews happily pointed out.

"Welp, I'm convinced. Let's head in," Baker keenly replied.

"Dispatch, show Twelve-Two clear on the last and heading in.", Andrews advised the dispatcher.

"Thank you Twelve-Two. We appreciate you, and I show you headed into the station," Dispatch replied.

"Thank you, Radio. Have a good New Years," Andrews responded.

"Thank you. You do the same. Stay safe," Dispatch replied.

Andrews makes a U-turn, slicing through the untouched snow.

"Whoa! Slow down cowboy. You're the only thing standing between me and my family. If we die because of your driving trying to make it in to off duty roll call, my wife is gonna kill you, and me!" Baker teased Andrews.

"Funny, Andrew Dice. I have everything under control. Plus, I'm scared of your wife," Andrews jested.

As they both laugh and continue telling jokes, Baker spots the described vehicle that they had been looking for, but never found.

"D.B., look," Andrews spoke with disappointment in his tone.

"Ahh man. Is that?" Baker paused with his question in disbelief.

"Looks like it. A tan minivan," Andrews reluctantly replied.

Both officers immediately noticed that the minivan that had been notoriously patrolling the area had no headlights on.

"Dammit!" Baker exclaimed. Aggressively, he picked up the microphone, "Radio, Twelve-Two."

"Go ahead Twelve-Two," Dispatch responded.

Officer Andrews gets in position behind the minivan, readying to affect a traffic stop.

"Yes, on our way into the station, we located that vehicle in the area of Adams and Main," Baker advised the dispatcher.

"Are you making a traffic stop of that vehicle," the dispatcher asked.

"Yes we are, Radio. Show us pulling over at Main and Tolbert. It's going to be a tan Chevy minivan, personalized license plate number T-O-N-E-L-O-C. Looks like it's occupied by about five individuals. We'll let you know," Baker relayed to dispatch.

"Okay, Twelve-Two. I have you on a traffic stop, investigating the minivan occupied times five. Cars in Twelve, Twelve-Two has a tan Chevy minivan, occupied five times under investigation at Main and Tolbert. If anyone is available to assist, you can make your way over there for a little backup," Dispatch responded.

As Twelve-Two pulled behind the minivan and came to a stop, Officer Andrews shined his spot light directly through the back of the darkened rear window, illuminating the inside as best as they could. That bright light also simultaneously made it harder for everyone inside of the vehicle to clearly see the officers behind them.

"Hold on for a second. Let's just sit here for a minute and see what they do," Andrews suggested.

"They're doing a lot of moving around in there," Officer Baker pointed out, making note that the occupants were making excessive and suspicious movements, possibly in preparation for some kind of eventful encounter.

Andrews relayed his concern, "I know. I don't want to just sit here any longer. This car is a coffin. We can't wait for backup in this weather."

Feeling antsy and lacking the proper illuminating equipment, both officers decide to exit their patrol car and establish contact.

"Let's get up there and do what we do. Just be ready just in case. Remember, the wife will kill us if we get killed," Baker jested once more.

Stepping out of the patrol car, both officers immediately noticed the effects of the pavement beneath their feet. Andrews slightly slipped because of the matted snow that turned into ice. Officer Baker stepped out of the passenger side door and into the welcoming tundra of deep snow that laid in wait.

Unfazed, both officers stay focused. Partners for a long time, they knew each other's moves intimately. More importantly, they trusted and relied on each other.

"Watch yourself, Drews," Baker warned his partner.

Andrews cautiously approached the driver's door, walking past the salt covered, deeply tinted windows that virtually wrapped around the entire vehicle.

"Copy that," he replied.

But as Andrews edged towards his uncertainty, Officer Baker soon found himself in an equally dangerous position.

Tactically approaching his own unknown from the passenger side. Baker had to keep an eye on traffic for his partner, who remained vulnerable in the street, his footing through the twelve inch high snow, opening the side sliding door and most importantly, keeping a sharp eye on every pair of hands inside of that rolling mini brigade of potential danger.

"Hello sir. I know it's cold out here, but we can hurry this up if you roll your window down a little so I can talk to you," Andrews explained to the driver who lowered his window only about a quarter of an inch.

"It's cold, sir," the young driver tragically pointed out.

"I realize that more than you do, because I'm standing out here while you're in there," Andrews replied with a build of both suspicion and contempt.

"I didn't ask you to pull me over," the driver intelligently decided to respond with.

"Ok, you can go ahead and turn your vehicle off, and then I'm gonna need your driver's license, insurance and registration, please," Andrews instructed.

"I didn't do anything, though. What did I do?" the young man foolishly continued.

Fed up and freezing, Andrews replied, "I'll tell you just as soon as you give me your driver's license, insurance and registration."

The driver then paused for a second and said, "I don't have any of that officer. It's in my wallet and I left it at home in my other pants."

Okay then, now I'm gonna need you to step out of the vehicle for me," Andrews instructed him.

Dismayed, the driver complied, stepping out explaining, "I was just driving them to the store to get ready to bring in the new year, Officer."

"That's fine," Andrews replied as he escorted him back to the patrol cruiser. "Go ahead and place your hands on the hood of the car for me."
"Please don't take me to jail, sir. I'll go home," the driver pleaded, placing his hands on the cold hood.

"We wouldn't be going through this if you had just cooperated. I was just gonna tell you to turn your headlights on and then advise you to go home because people are calling on you, saying that you're driving around this area recklessly. Now I have to check you and everybody in that ride," Andrews explained as he searched the driver for weapons.

"I don't have anything on me, Sir," the young man explained.

"Great. Is there anything in the vehicle that me and my partner should know about? That is your vehicle, right?" Andrews inquired.

"No sir. I mean yes, sir. I mean no, there's nothing in there. It's my van but it's in my mother's name. Officer, we were just going to the store," he nervously replied.

Andrews pulled out his cuffs and explained to the driver, "You are not under arrest. These are for your safety and my safety, alright?"

"Yes sir," the driver replied.

Andrews went on to explain, "I just need to, at the very least, confirm your identity with my computer and write your name down as someone that I had contact with today, ok?"

With a new outlook on his current New Year situation, the young driver's challenging demeanor adjusted accordingly.

"Yes sir and I want to apologize for making your job hard, Officer. I just want to go home," he explained.

Meanwhile, on the other side of the minivan, Baker's hurdling circumstances were just starting.

"Sir, I need you to unlock your door, please," Baker asked the front seat passenger, whom had already rolled his window completely down.

Uncertain of what was awaiting him on the other side of that sliding door, Baker draws his weapon, making sure to keep it pointed in a downward direction.

In complete compliance, the front passenger slowly reached down to unlock the door. Immediately, Officer Baker pulled the handle and slid the rear door open.

Instantaneously, Baker got a bad feeling. Standing in snow that towered above the top of his boots, he pulled one foot free from the limiting hazard and took a step backwards, gaining a better balanced footing.

He raised his weapon to a forty-five degree angle, intentionally avoiding taking aim and assuming a target. His thought was to let every occupant of that vehicle know that he was determined to actualize any of their misguided ideas if it ever came down to it.

With no lighting from their shoulders down, the lower half of the interior of the minivan was pitch black. Although there were only four occupants instead of five, Baker quickly realized that he still had a serious handicap with his ability to visually secure the condition of everyone's hands.

"I'm gonna need everybody to place their hands on the seat in front of you," he told them. "Front passenger, you can place your hands on the dashboard. Just keep them there for now and don't move for me. As soon as my partner is done with your friend over there, everyone can go about the rest of their day and we can all enjoy our New Year."

Either in agreeance or through intimidation, all four young men happily complied.

But as Baker stood there, waiting. He had a funny feeling that someone in that tan Chevy minivan wasn't quite right. As those few moments past, waiting for his partner to place the driver into the backseat of the patrol car, Baker's suspicion became more and more focused on the passenger positioned in the most rear seat of the vehicle. After several reminders and warnings to hold still and keep his hands in plain sight on the seat in front of him, that one singled out individual quickly became Baker's sole focus.

With a compliant occupant seated in the front and an extremely cagey passenger seated in the third row, a very large man wearing only a t-shirt and a pair of blue jeans with sandals was positioned in the second row, impeding further progress. It was an obstacle that needed addressing.

"Second row passenger, step out and walk over to my partner at the hood of my car," Baker instructed.

Again, with no sign of aggression, malice or any other kind of underhandedness, Baker kept the majority of his focus on the third row passenger.

Andrews met the second row seated passenger in between the two vehicles and ordered him to place his hands on the hood.

After the complete search for any offensive weapons and or contraband, the passenger immediately asked Andrews, "Do I have to stand out here? It's kinda cold. Can I at least sit in the back of your car while you do your thing?"

Knowing that the passenger couldn't go back into the minivan just yet, and that it would be inhuman to make the underdressed large man freeze while they complete their investigation, Andrews had no problem with the request.

"Only under one condition. I'm gonna have to place cuffs on you if you want to sit back there," Andrews replied.

"Deal, this is too much for me," the large man exclaimed.

Now, with two of the occupants secured in the backseat of the patrol unit, Baker can now scratch the itch that had been bothering him that entire time.

"Alright guy. Seeing as though you can't comprehend the concept of being still, it's your turn, step out," Baker instructed him.

As Andrews shut the back door of their scout car, Baker prepared for anything as the fidgety backseat passenger began to exit.

Predictably, the suspicious passenger unnecessarily removed his hands from the seat in front of him, lowering them into the limbo-like darkness that blanketed the entire bottom half of the interior. Purposely bending downward, submerging eighty percent of his body into a void of light, there was a moment that gave birth to Baker's thought process of possibly ending this young man's life.

Baker immediately raised his gun, taking aim...

"Hands! Hands! Let me see your hands!" Baker repeated as the young man stood to his feet and stepped out into the thick snow.

With a mindless aggressive motion, the seemingly doomed passengers' momentum stepping down and out of the minivan caused him to appear that he was about to enter Officer Baker's personal space.

Baker instantly raised his open free hand toward the young man's chest while simultaneously raising his weapon, pointing it directly in his face.

"Whoa!" Baker exclaimed with authority. "You might want to rethink your next move, bro. Accident or not; this won't end well for you."

Realizing his mistake, the young man just raised his hands, but the look on his face, along with how he reacted, or the lack there of, spoke volumes to Baker. Not saying anything about what just happened, peeked Baker's interest even more, confirming his suspicion that this guy was riding around dirty.

"Just walk over there with to my partner and put your hands on the hood. It's as simple as that," Baker calmly explained while noticing the erratic man pier over his shoulder, appearing to search for a path to run.

Again, with his hands raised and without saying a word, the uncooperative passenger, complied, but his uncanny inability to follow direction would soon prove to be superior to his common sense.

"Watch this one, partner! He's squirrelly!" Baker shouts to Andrews.

Stepping out of the deep snow, the suspicious man quickly finds his footing on the slippery matted snowy pavement. Andrews stood at the driver side headlight, waiting for the young man to walk over and place his hands on the hood, but again, no ability to follow directions.

"You can just place your hands right there," Andrews told him.

As he began lowering his hands down onto the hood, desperate stupidity kicked in. Using the elements to his advantage, the daring man ran, continuing on the path between the two vehicles, pushing past Andrews, causing him to slip.

Andrews steadied himself with the scout car and quickly regained his balance. He immediately turned and gave chase.

Meanwhile, Officer Baker still had an issue. With one more passenger remaining in the vehicle, options were thin. He couldn't leave the unsecured man in the minivan and he couldn't let his partner chase that, now perpetrator, by himself. Then there were the other two that were already in the back of the patrol unit.

He immediately aimed in. "Don't move!" Baker shouted to the remaining passenger.

"I'm not moving," he replied with fear, not knowing what was transpiring behind him.

Andrews soon caught up to the slippery fleeing subject. He instinctively stretched out to grab him by the shoulders. That's when the determined man slowed his flight, turned completely around and used Officer Andrew's zealous momentum that naturally built in pursuit, against him. Grabbing him by his arms, the perpetrator manage to throw Andrews to the ground, stumbling down to the pavement along with him.

Although the use of that particular law of physics assisted the uncooperative man in the struggle to shake Officer Andrews off of him, he would soon discover that there was more than one law in physics.

The perpetrator quickly jumped to his feet, then there was this unique and unmistakable, "clank." As he took two strides, he instantly realized that the "clank" sound that echoed off of the nearby building was actually his gun that jarred loose because of the impact of the ground when he fell, stringing the one spot that had exposed concrete.

"Don't do it! Don't do it!" Andrews shouted as he pulled his weapon out and aimed in.

That was the exact moment when the frustrating young man's knack for failing to follow commands would turn out to be his ultimate demise.

With a foolish and unmanaged thought, the young man stopped in his tracks, turned around, paused to think about it, and sprinted back towards the fallen weapon.

Disregarding Officer Andrews and his command, the third row passenger picked up the gun and turned away to continue his escape, but when he turned, he pointed that same weapon directly at Officer Andrews.

Just like that. Just that quick. Just that easy.

With one shot, a man's life ended with a bullet directly to the heart.

Officer Baker attempted to pull out his hand radio to transmit what was happening, but the clip that was supposed to be secured to the back of it, snapped off. Causing it to fall; swallowed and lost somewhere in the foot-plus deep snow.

"Ok, I quit," the deceptive armed man said after immediately collapsing to the ground.

Officer Andrews was left with no other option, but to discharge his weapon, in order to keep his promise to his partner and family to make it back home at the end of his shift.

With all of that happening so fast, all Officer Baker had a chance to do in the meantime, was to stay aimed in on the front passenger and watch what was transpiring right in front of his eyes, as if it were a live tragic documentary. Once the chaos ended, Baker immediately opened the front passenger side door.

"Get out!" Baker yelled with urgency.

He threw the last passenger down into the heavy snow and quickly placed his first pair of cuffs on him.

"Stay there!" Baker told him, leaving him to lay in the deep December snow.

Officer Baker sprinted over to the downed man not knowing if he was actually struck by the instinctive shot from his partner. He kicked the perps gun away and hurriedly placed his second pair of cuffs on him.

"Stay down!" he ordered him.

But as he rolled him over, he knew it was too late. The defiant man was gone.

"Drews, are you okay?" Baker inquired with concern.

Obviously in shock and still aimed in as if he were stuck in that position, Andrews could only answer with, "Yeah."

"Call it out. I don't have my radio," Baker told his partner.

Although Andrews contacted dispatch and transmitted the emergency priority that had just took place, he never lowered his weapon.

"Drews," Baker called out as he carefully walked over to him. "Are you okay, brother?"

"I'm good," Andrews insisted.

Still on a strategic approach, Baker reached outward. "You're still aimed in, brother."

"Oh," Andrews replied with a distant puzzled look on his face.

"Let me hold that for you. The sirens are getting louder. Backup is almost here," Baker suggested out of a building concern.

Snapping out of it, Andrews realized that he was still aimed in, and immediately handed his service weapon over to him until he could get himself back together.

Once backup, EMS and supervision arrived, Andrews began to resemble his former self. Although, over the course of the next few months, normal for either Officer Andrews or Officer Baker would relentlessly become an unforeseen struggle.

As if it were that bad documentary movie stuck on repeat, Officer Baker would suffer night terrors, dreaming of several outcomes born of that fatal night, for months.

For Officer Andrews, life changed. With bad media coverage that misrepresent and twisted facts about the incident, along with the family filing a wrongful death suit, a drawn out internal investigation, almost dying and the thriving actuality of taking a life, being trapped in his own mind was proving to be the worst place for him, quickly.

Almost an entire year later, these two brave officers were completely cleared of any and all wrong doing by both Internal Affairs as well as in civil court. Officers Baker and Andrews eventually returned to full duty and even though the actions taken by those officers on that New Year's Eve were legitimate, they will naturally continue to struggle with that night for a very long time to come.

-CONCLUSION-

This was a case where the two officers displayed keen diligence in their readiness. Although they received a seemingly simple police run, their shift and year were both nearing an end, and the constant battle with the treacherous elements raged on, tagging in and out throughout the entire ordeal, Officers Andrews and Baker successfully preformed their duties without prejudice or failure.

In the performance and pursuit of enforcing the law, officers inevitably discover that the living definition of the job demand poise, professionalism and proficiency. These three characteristics directly affect the outcome of every circumstance that can transpire throughout a career. But officers are not robots.

Although those three enduring aspects are needed, human beings are built with more programing than that. It is that condition that makes human beings so successful throughout life. Instinct, compassion and fear are some of the other indispensable and distinguishing values that were displayed by both officers in this story. They too, played a major role in the outcome.

Though victims of pressure from unrelenting investigations, targeting style media coverage and other outside distractions, officers should never shy away, but vigorously seek help when needed. After all, we're only human.

CHAPTER / sixteen

Child's Play

Growing up in an unresting environment, a person reserves the right to a developed affinity for the understanding of their surroundings. Either pampered by the infamous parental bubble of protection or hardened by the welcoming arms of the street, the craft of relation can quickly become a formidable ally.

Short of championing a Phd in psychology, police officers are charged with arriving at an issue, determining its origin and then effectively deploying a resolution that is impartial and equally beneficial on a daily basis.

As you will read, there will come times when those calculating efforts are put to the test with high risk stakes.

-CASEHISTORY-

Already molded with tons of experience by the constant battle of the streets, Officer Gregory Stone was known to walk with a big stick. Assigned to handle the youth crimes in the district for the past nine and a half years, Stone had affectionately earned a reputation to effectively police the ever dangerous and highly confrontational, natural enemy to any authority... the average teenager.

Formally a member of the departments' gang enforcement unit, Officer Stone had been working with children and their individual problems in and out of schools, homes and streets with such a vigorous and passionate drive for so long, that he was bestowed the nickname, "Uncle."

Gang members feared him, teachers relied on him, parents respected him and the students needed him.

Officer Stone prided himself on being down to earth and approachable. He had an open door policy and a well-known effective set of rules. Nicknamed "The three biblical rules of Stone," they were a simple and unforgettable high school set of student body laws that made each child accountable for themselves and their own success. The first rule was to always speak with respect to one another. The second one was to maintain a functional level of a personal daily hygiene. Lastly, and considered to most students as the most important one of them all, was to never force him to take any kind of official police action. If anyone was to ever break any of the "Three biblical rules of Stone," they would quickly come to regret it, wishing that their parents would have found out instead of "Uncle."

But there's always that one student, delinquent juvenile or plain old rebellious child that would mysteriously be stricken by the chip on the shoulder virus. They tend to become delusional and brave, foolishly deciding to test their limits with Officer Stone and his notorious rules. Needless to say, once they became reeducated on the natural order of things, the unstable stand on their misguided policies were quickly vacated.

Partially through the seemingly endless hours of a school day, Officer Stone was making his way through his routine rounds, checking in on his assigned schools in the district when he received a call on his cell phone from the Vice Principal of a school that he was already on his way to at that moment

Officer Stone answered. "VP Sanders, how are you, ma'am?" he inquired.

"I'm doing wonderful today and yourself?" she responded.

"I'm okay, thank you. Ready for the day to come to a peaceful ending at any moment now. What can I help you with?" Stone asked.

The VP quickly got to the point. "I just received some information that there were a group of tenth graders that where seen skipping class, and hiding out in a stairwell at an entrance, located somewhere in the rear of the school," she mentioned. "Could you take care of that for us? We'd very much appreciate it," she continued.

"No Problem Ms. Sanders, I was on my way over there anyway. I should be pulling up shortly, and I'll make sure that that'll be the first thing I check on," he assured her.

Grateful, the vice principle expressed her gratitude. "Thank you, Officer Stone. I'm headed over there right now myself. I'll meet you there," she notified him.

Disappointed with a dash of frustration, Officer Stone pulled into the school's teacher parking lot that was tucked away in the rear of the school. Well into the school year, Stone knows for a fact that all of the students are personally familiar with the, "Three biblical rules of Stone." So he naturally viewed the situation as possible outsiders, or a false report.

As Stone exited his scout car, he could hear the loud and unruly voices of several teens coming from just inside of the employee doors. He walked over to the exterior doors that led to an interior stairwell on a mission to check out what exactly the delinquent students were doing.

"Shit! Here comes Stone!" one of the lookout students announced as he shut the partially opened exterior door.

A group of eight students, they all panic, attempted to discard their paraphernalia and collectively decide to head in the only way they can to get as far away from Officer Stone. Problem is, they were headed right for the assistant principle and the school's security guards.

As they turned and ran up the five steps that led back into the school, they soon realized that they were trapped. Trapped between a rock and a very hard place.

With no plan B, and no other way of escape, the troubling teenagers quickly abandon their feeble attempt to flee. Instead, a rebellious few decide to pick up another form of adolescent protest, direct insurrection.

"What are you students doing in my hallways and not in class?" the Assistant Principal aggressively questioned.

But before they could answer, the other shoe fell. Like the first day as an inmate condemned to a twenty year stint inside of Rikers Island, the turning of the lock on the exterior door began to rotate. Click by click, the individual clinking sounds of the seemingly slow-motion turning gears in the lock, echoed through the hallway with a deafening effect.

Unable to answer the Assistant Principal's questions due to the distraction of a certain end, the few rebellious, became even fewer. In an imminent fear of Officer Stone's justice for their near foreseen future, all eight students turned around with a frightening anticipation.

The powerful smell of cigarettes slapped Officer Stone square in the face as soon as he entered the corridor. "Who's been up in here smoking?" Stone loudly questioned as he opened the door to walk in.

Completely shook, the group of misfits misplace their brazen ideals and cower, all except for one.

"What do we have here?" Stone asked rhetorically.

"We..."

"Did I tell you to talk?" Stone interrupted one of the doomed students. "Nope, stop. Don't answer that. We both know the response." He abruptly commented. "All of you, line up, single file. And I think that there's no need for me to remind any of you not to say a word."

The teens lined up and await their fate with an extremely uncomfortable anticipation.

The schools' security guards began to confiscate all of the students' I.D. cards.

As Officer Stone walked over to speak to Ms. Sanders, the one determined delinquent decided to make himself known.

With all of the students lined up facing away from Ms. Sanders and Officer Stone, he spoke. "How long do we have to stand here looking stupid?" he asked in a low, but audible tone.

Shocked at the nerve on display, Stone quickly turned around. "Who said that?" he asked.

No one answered.

"Really? That's how we're gonna play it?" Stone asked sarcastically. "Tell you what, the first person to speak up can go right back to class like this never happened," he offered.

That's when it happened. The very brave, but extremely foolish student decided to take his journey to a whole other level. Officer Stone stood there, bearing witness to the unfortunate young soul, take one hand and place it into his right pocket, attempting to pull something out. But Stone is positioned on the left side of the students and can't clearly see what was going on.

Now there are metal detectors at every student entrance, but each one of those students still had access to the outside for who knows how long before being discovered.

Stone immediately puts his hand on his gun. "What are you doing, son? Take your hands out of your pockets! Do it, right now!" he shouted.

As if he were oblivious to Officer Stone's commands, the young man continued on his expedition. The young man slightly bent over to his left.

Officer Stone unsnapped his weapon. "Stop right now, son!" he shouted as the other kids became even more nervous.

Still unfazed, the determined youth continued on with his reckless plot.

Stone started to pull his weapon out. Slowly, steadily, inch by inch, Officer Stone reluctantly drug his weapon from its comfort zone.

Then, the disturbed young man stood upright with his hand close to his face and lit a cigarette. He took a long puff and exhaled. "I said it," he admitted as he raised his hand. "Can I go back to class now? That *is* what you said."

In total shock, coupled with a side of irritation, Stone slammed his gun back into his holster and dismissed everyone else, but the Marlboro boy.

"Boy, I almost killed you! Are you on that stuff? Huh?" Stone yells.

With no response, the delusional young man takes a smooth and even longer puff. He exhaled again and answered, "Nope. You?"

In an almost uncontrollable rage, Officer Stone snatched the cigarette out of the boys hand, threw it to the floor and ground it into the linoleum.

"Yeah, you ready. Let's go. March your little ignorant butt out to my car and do not pass go!" Stone instructed the boy. "Ms. Sanders, I apologize if I overstepped, but he has to go," he explained.

"I understand Officer Stone. I'll walk with you out there," she volunteered. "Could one of you guys go and get his file?" Sanders asked the schools' security.

"Yes ma'am," they answer as they take his I.D. to the front office to retrieve his information.

"What's your name, son?" Stone asked the unidentified student as they walked down the hallway back towards the stairwell.

"I ain't yo son? You can kill all that, Bro," he replied.

First off, I'm not your buddy or your bro. You can call me Officer or Officer Stone, and when you tell me your name, then I'll address you accordingly," Stone responded.

Remaining silent, the stubborn teen inched his back pack tighter to his shoulder and lowered his head.

"Now you're gonna get quiet all of a sudden? That's cool. It's probably best for the both of us, because I'm not trying to lose my job over you," Stone explained to him.

"Man, whatever, Bro," the deliberate teen verbally jabbed once more.

Stone stopped halfway down the stairwell, turned around, and just as he stepped towards the, now mortally endangered teen, Ms. Sanders quickly stepped in.

"Officer Stone! We'll get you his information," Sanders intervened. "Let's just wait right here until they come back with what we need," she suggested, thinking that Officer Stone would possibly break a few laws along with a few bones if left alone with the obviously disturbed youth.

Standing at the last step, Officer Stone stared at the teen with an enormous amount of contempt.

"What are you looking at?" the young man questioned Officer Stone. He then turned to the Assistant Principal standing at the top of the stairs, "Ms. Sanders. I feel very uncomfortable right now."

"Boy, be quiet. Ain't nobody gonna touch you," Stone said to the teen.

He turned back towards the officer, "They said you like little boys. Now I know the truth," the teen continued with his taunt.

Observing that the student was crossing the line, Ms. Sanders interjected. "Young man that is enough. You are being extremely rude and it is uncalled for. Now I know your mother and father have taught you to act better than a common hooligan with no upbringing. You're making us all look bad," she scolded.

"I don't care. I'mma do me, you do you!" the incorrigible teen spouted.

Understanding that they were not going to get anywhere with the young man while he was obviously upset and intending to lash out, both Officer Stone and Ms. Sanders decided to temporarily suspend their verbal interaction with the teen.

"Ms. Sanders, this is Officer Grimes. The students name is going to be Maurice Anderson. We'll be back over there in a minute with a copy of his file for you." security transmitted to Ms. Sanders over her radio.

"Let's just wait for the rest of his file and I'll be happy to get him out of your hair," Stone told Sanders.

"Why wait? Let's go right now. I'm tired of being here anyway," the teen suggested.

"I'm not sure what you're aiming for here, Mr. Anderson, but I promise you this, you will not accomplish it," Officer Stone explained.

"You think?" Maurice rudely replied.

"Maurice. I know you're better than this," Sanders pointed out.

"Lady, you don't know me. You didn't even know my name until somebody else told you. Both of y'all walk around this school like y'all doin' somthin'. Here's a news flash; both of y'all can go to hell on a flammable horse," Maurice responded with his continued insulting retort as he chose to voluntarily enter the point of no return by placing his size eleven shoe on Officer Stone's knee that was resting just on a step below him.

In that instant, Officer Stone, known for his defining aggressive response, caught himself. It was at that point that he knew that this kid was lost and looking for attention and possibly more.

Ms. Sanders was in complete shock. With disgust in his demeanor and concern for his safety, she remained speechless and unable to counter the fifteen year olds' disrespectful maneuver.

"Ok Mr. Anderson. I see you," Stone metaphorically responded with a calming toned disposition.

"See what?" Maurice asked as his face simultaneously began to change from anger to vulnerability. His head turned away from Stone as a revealing tear is reluctantly freed from its watery prison. "I told y'all. You don't know me. So there ain't nothin' for you to see, Officer Stone," he rebelliously continued.

It was at that specific moment that Stone knew without question. Legitimized by past experiences, he pierced the boy's destructive facade, recognizing that he had just called out for help. See, along with the vulnerable youth's tears, Maurice had just acknowledged Officer Stone by his actual name.

Officer Stone took a step towards Maurice. With the uncertainty of Stones intentions, Ms. Sanders instinctively inhales, desperately in search for her composure.

He extended his hand. "My name is Officer Gregory Stone. Nice to meet you," he told him, reintroducing himself to the young man.

Maurice hesitated. He was confused and thrown off. Puzzled, but slowly beginning to understand, he looks at Officer Stone's hand and then into his eyes, searching for clarity. As he attempted to dissect the completely foreign gesture, Maurice cautiously raised his open hand, extending it out to Officer Stone, eventually shaking it with a much needed heartfelt relief.

Filled with an uncontrollable amount of emotion that he just couldn't hold on to any longer, Maurice completely broke down, melting into Officer Stone's arms and like a flood gate, he let go and released a powerful and revealing amount of his emotional torture.

Stone extended his arms outward. "I got you, we got you," he assured Maurice.

But just as Officer Stone tightened his much needed hug of the emotionally broken young man, Maurice let out a grunt.

Almost immediately, Stone loosened his grip, "You ok? I didn't hurt you, did I?" Stone asked as he released him, placing his hands on Maurice's shoulders.

Maurice let out another grunt. This time, he quickly pulled away.

That's when Stone saw it. A bruise that stretched from the back of his neck towards his shoulder, retreating underneath his shirt.

As if Maurice's emotions were contagious, Officer Stone fought hard to hold back the lone tear that eventually broke free, slowly descending down his face. Because he too, was once a victim to similar circumstances, the situation at hand instantly became personal.

Beyond pissed, Stone assured Maurice, "From now on, I'm at your disposal. I'm gonna take care of this. I told you, I got you."

After everything that transpired at the birth of their meeting, Officer Stone decided to understand and forgive Maurice. He eventually made arrangements to drive the in need teen to a nearby relative before making a quick home visit to a certain, deserving, individual.

After notifying his supervisors as well as other appropriate notifications, Stone held true to his word and arrested the abused teen's father for child abuse along with any other additional charges they could find for him.

After an extensive investigation, it was discovered that the father was abusing, both Maurice and his mother. It was so bad, that Maurice found the abhorrent behavior to be normal and would often follow his father's example, regularly disrespecting women, including his mother.

Over the next year or so, Officer Stone would routinely take time out of his work day to check in on Maurice, counseling him whenever needed.

Rough in the beginning, Officer Stone ventured above and beyond in saving the young man's mind and future. Now having to mature faster, Stone pointed out the difficulty in the tireless balancing act of a double edge sword.

Encouraging Maurice to excel and develop an original outlook on life for himself, Stone reiterated the importance in discarding the earlier, loathsome proclivities learned throughout his childhood; while at the same time, encouraging Maurice to retain the core lessons learned from those same repulsively dysfunctional experiences.

Officer Stone was also able to explain and teach Maurice the importance of his counterpart. Pointing out the fact that treating women the way that he had observed most of his young life was unacceptable. Using his mother as a starting point, Stone explained that women deserved devoted respect. He reinforced the moral principle by educating Maurice that his mother, as does every mother, unselfishly and extraordinarily, place their own lives in a fifty/ fifty jeopardy during child birth, and that there will forever be a looming and unwritten lifelong debt to his mother and every other female that he would encounter throughout his life. Whether he asked for it or not.

Maurice and Officer Stone lost touch with each other just before his high school graduation and hadn't seen each other for about five years, until Maurice spotted Stone on a police run in his old neighborhood. When Maurice walked up to Officer Stone, Stone didn't even recognize him at all. The incorrigible delinquent had become a grown man. They quickly reintroduced themselves to each other. This time, Maurice took it easy on his old Bro and eventually caught up over drinks later that night.

Now, a college graduate and successful business owner, Maurice Anderson continues to be a productive citizen, taking care of his mother who now resides with him. She, his wife, and his two children, all remain his unwavering devotion. Maurice remains one of Officer Stone's most valuable and treasured investments in his often thankless job.

-CONCLUSION-

This chapter entered into a realm of dire conclusions. With such high consequences at stake, officers must evaluate their circumstances case by case, with impartial effectiveness every time they act in their official capacity. Used efficiently, this practice can spill over into their personal life, reducing conflict at home as well as on the job.

This tale of truths also provide evidence that the chosen career of the selfless and courageous can result in immeasurable reward. Some acknowledged and some not.

CHAPTER / seventeen

Not Safe, Not Yet

Although there will come times during an officers' tenure served in law enforcement, where a certain sense of comfort can desperately be needed, it can also quickly become the number one culprit to the most fatal indiscretion an individual can make.

A natural paralytic to the state of perceptive alertness, comfort can be an enemy that is often unconsciously welcomed into conversation, routine procedure, work performances and situational environments. Habit forming, it easily possesses a threat to our everyday lives. Comfort can take away that certain edge needed for that moment, the effort called for in professionalism, or even that one particularly significant step that routinely helps to keep you and your partner maintained and free from danger.

-CASE HISTORY-

It was a late April, spring morning. Officer Kevin Bailey awoke early to take care of a few chores before he was off to work for the day. He had been working a ton of overtime so that he could surprise his two little girls with the news of going to Disney Land over the summer. The overtime took time away from his family, so he was especially excited at the thought of springing the good news to them that morning.

Bailey finished up with his chores and made some breakfast for them before they headed off to school. As they all sat down to enjoy their meal, he boiled over with anticipation of their reactions.

He apologized for his recent absenteeism and explained that he knew that he hadn't been around as much lately and that all the work that he was putting in was all for them. As he continued breaking the news to his two daughters, he could see their faces light up like two lanterns in the dark of night.

Emphatically excited, his two daughters lost their minds. One of them began dancing around in little circles and the other smiled and started to cry uncontrollably. So far, Officer Bailey's day was going great and he felt like it couldn't turn out any better, but what he didn't realize was that his day hadn't even begun yet.

As Bailey pulled into the district parking lot that morning, his content and happy demeanor inexplicably changed. He began to experience a buildup of an uneasy feeling. It was undeniable, yet unexplainable. Was it something he ate or just a sudden sense of caution that came over him? Whatever it was, Bailey couldn't shake it.

One more goodbye over the phone to his family, assuring them that he'd be home after his regular shift as he walked into the station. Just as he hung the phone up, Bailey looked up and noticed a young woman seated in the front lobby that had obviously been crying and still seemed visibly upset. He continued on with his preparation for roll call, but still couldn't shake that irrefutable nagging feeling.

As Bailey and his partner, Officer Frederick Rogers, received their assignments and the daily activities, they walked back into the front lobby and quickly realize that the young woman was still there.

Officer Bailey approached the supervisor on the desk and asked, "Excuse me Lieutenant, but what's up with that lady sitting on the bench in the lobby?"

"Bailey! Just the man I've been looking for. I need you to take care of this for me. She is here because she wants to get her baby daughter back. She stated that while she was at that McDonald's restaurant up the street, a man walked up to her child, picked her up out of her stroller and walked out," the Lieutenant explained.

"Really?" Bailey replied in astonishment.

"Yes, and I need you and Rogers to take care of that right off of the ramp. Dispatch already has you busy on it."

"Copy that," Bailey replied.

Rogers and Bailey walked over to the distraught mother with the average assumption that the situation was more than likely some sort of domestic, baby-daddy drama, but after introducing themselves and then hearing her story, they quickly realized that they could not be further from the truth. What she appeared to be describing turned out to be an actual kidnapping.

As Rogers and Bailey gathered all of the pertinent information that they needed to proceed with their investigation, she mentioned that she followed the strange man to the house where he was keeping her daughter. Immediately, Officer Bailey was struck by an almost out of body experience. A kind of numbness came over him as the blood seemed to have rushed out of his body all at once. His mind raced as he could only imagine the many different scenarios of how this situation could play out.

Rogers wrote down the address as Bailey stocked the car with the required daily equipment. They advised the mother to stay at the station, notified dispatch and then hurried over to the location that was only a half of a mile away from the district. While on the way, Bailey's mind continued to race with disastrous thoughts. He couldn't imagine anything more nerve racking than the concept of not knowing the condition of your own child. It was a situation that he wouldn't wish on anyone.

The April morning ushered in thick dreary rain clouds, but strangely hadn't produced much rain fall. It was as if the weather was waiting for the perfect moment to bring even more gloom to a day that had begun on such a high note for Officer Bailey.

As Rogers and Bailey arrived to the address, Bailey noticed a narcotic raid van that passed by as he and Rogers exited their patrol car. Bailey waved hello, realizing that he knew a few of the raid crew that passed by.

Rogers on the other hand immediately focused in on the home realizing that the stairwell to the front porch seemed awkwardly narrow. They lead to a two family flat with a door to the right and the other on the left.

"Partner, this is about to get very interesting," Rogers stated knowing that the slim stairwell created a natural fatal funnel.

"I see. Watch yourself," Bailey replied with a conscious warning.

With no other recourse, they made their way up the steps, announcing themselves so as not to be suddenly compromised by the poor tactical positioning.

Noticing that the apartment door to the left was partially opened, Bailey and Rogers made their way towards it. They could hear voices coming from the inside. Unable to make out the faint sound clearly, Officer Bailey cautiously pushed the slightly ajar door open even further.

Again, they announce themselves, "Police! We are coming in."

Just as the door completely opened, Bailey could see a shirtless man standing in the living room, clutching a young child tightly to his chest, almost like the baby was his personal human shield. They immediately recognize a man fitting the description of the male who took the distraught woman's child. Seated across the room crying, was an older woman, believed to be the shirtless man's mother.

With his partner to his left and closest to the door, Bailey walked closer and introduced himself. "Hello." He said in a calming tone. "I'm Officer Bailey and this is my partner, Officer Rogers. We received a call to come check on you guys. Just making sure everything was alright."

With only a dead stare, the unknown man refused to respond. Bailey could instantaneously see that this man was not willing to reason and was more than likely going to be problematic.

As Rogers grabbed his mic to his radio in order to provide dispatch with an update, the man became infuriated and started screaming at him, "What are you calling backup for? You came into my house and now you need backup? I think it would be best for you if you turn your white ass back around and go back the way you came!" he aggressively warned.

It was at that time that Bailey took the opportunity to place his radio into his left hand just behind his hip as he canted his body. Now, hidden out of the shirtless irate man's sight, Bailey pressed down on his radios' button, keying the mic and opening up a one way transmission so that everyone monitoring could hear what was transpiring and possibly render assistance.

"Sir, hey now," Bailey chimed in, attempting to press the reset on the man's building rage. "Talk to me. I can help you solve all of this real fast. Just let me have the baby, so that she doesn't accidentally get hurt, okay. She doesn't need to be exposed to all of this yelling."

"I'm not doing shit! You want this baby? You come and take it!" he aggressively replied.

"At least let me make sure she's okay," Bailey pleaded.

"What did I just say?" he sarcastically asked.

Exhausted from the man's bravado, Rogers pulled out his can of mace.

"If you spray me with that, I'mma take your gun and shoot your white ass in the face!" the man threatened furiously.

Continuing to attempt to calm the situation, Bailey used every type of psychological trick he could think of to safely bring the volatile powder keg to a conclusion. But as he continued with his negotiation tactics, he was able to observe more of his surroundings, noticing that he was standing in a living room full of US Marine Corp memorabilia. Suddenly, the situation took on a potentially different view.

Are these even real? Are these his service accreditations? What are they for? Does he specialize in something they need to be aware of? Is this person suffering from PTSD?

It was the quick thinking that Bailey had done earlier, that seemed to have done the trick. Another scout responded to their hostile run.

"Police Officers, coming in!" they shouted.

In walked two different officers, but this time, one of them happened to be the same race as the shirtless subject. It was at that moment that the deranged man changed his entire disposition.

Bailey immediately noticed the difference and strategically stepped back. K n o w i n g t h e dynamics of what was actually transpiring with the run because of the opened transmission, the same raced officer entered with a refreshing calm.

"What's up?" he calmly asked.

"We're just talking about the baby. Just want to check on her," Bailey replied.

"Oh, is that all?" the officer responded. He then looked over to the shirtless man, still holding on to the young baby girl and explained, "Man, just give me the baby and we can end all of this. Looks like you got your mom over there upset and worried. Not to mention, I know she wants us out of her lovely home."

Then, the craziest thing happened. Just like that, the man decided to release the baby, but he threw the infant to the officer like she was a pillow being tossed onto a couch. Fortunately, the officer caught the baby girl and she turned out to be completely unharmed.

They placed the shirtless kidnapper into handcuffs as Rogers asked the older woman that was obviously relieved that the arrested man didn't get hurt during the confrontation, to retrieve a shirt for the man before being transported. Meanwhile Bailey walked the subject out to their vehicle to place him in the rear of their patrol unit, but there was one issue. Their patrol car wasn't equipped with a dividing shield. So now, Officer Bailey and the now arrested shirtless man had to stand outside for a couple of extra minutes to wait for the other responding unit to open their back door, so that he could be placed in there instead. The time spent out in the light drizzling rain seemed to annoy the shirtless kidnapper. It wasn't long until the other unit opened the door, but it must've been too long for him.

On the way out, Rogers brought the other unit's car keys and the shirt for their subject, so that he would have something to wear in lockup. Officer Bailey placed their perpetrator into the back seat with no issues whatsoever. Relieved, all Bailey could think to himself was that he was glad that it was safe and all over, and that no one got hurt. Then, as he leaned into the patrol unit to place the shirt over the still cuffed man's head, the subject head butted Bailey square in his face.

Painfully startled, Bailey jumped up and staggered backwards desperately grasping for something, anything, to grab on to in order to prevent himself from falling. With blood now gushing out of his eyes and nose, he found himself struggling to breathe or see clearly. As he stumbled backward, Bailey was just able to blindly find the push bar of his patrol unit which was parked just behind Seven-Seven's vehicle. He managed to reach for his radio with one hand and pulled himself close to the hood with the other. Beginning to lose consciousness, Bailey was just able to key his radio and yell for help. It was at that moment that he collapsed onto the hood of his patrol car, rapidly passing out. Just as his eyes closed, Bailey could hear the distant sound of police sirens and screeching tires, but all he could envision was the smiles on his two beautiful daughter's faces from earlier that morning.

After being transported to the hospital, Bailey awoke with his wife and those same two beautiful daughters standing over him. His partner, Rogers soon walked in and notified him that although the perpetrator attempted to get away, he was still in custody thanks to the raid crew that Bailey had seen earlier and returned to help. He went on to explain that the shirtless kidnapper, suffering from PTSD, was an actual US Marine veteran who was trained how to incapacitate, and even kill someone using such a devastating attack.

The arrested kidnapper was eventually charged with kidnapping and aggravated assault of a police officer. Officer Bailey suffered devastating injuries that required two surgeries on his right eye and an additional two on his nose, but was eventually able to return back to work with minimal complications.

-CONCLUSION-

Familiarity has the potential to breed comfort. In this case, the actions demonstrated by the perpetrator towards the conclusion of this encounter leaned more in the direction of a calming demeanor with situational understanding, but when dealing with the public, an officer should never make any assumptions that call for a deescalating defensive mindset. Therefore, it is incumbent for every law enforcement officer to always remain attentive to their situational circumstance.

CHAPTER / eighteen

<u>End of Tour</u>

Law enforcement is a courageous career choice to brave. If chosen, policing can offer a rewarding path in life. Although it can, at times, resemble something like an emotional roller coaster, this profession can help rewrite the lives of everyone you encounter, making the practice of law enforcement one of the most humanistic and morally coveted professions in the world.

Officers pride themselves on courage, honor, integrity and compassion. Lacking these essential governing qualities while wielding such a seductively authoritative power can be the determining factors between a good and bad police officer....although the road to consciously apply them without prejudice is a never ending endeavor within the making of a great police officer.

"Nearly all men can stand adversity, but if you want to test a man's character, give him power."
- ABRAHAM LINCOLN

The constant and erroneous practices of the overcharging and the inequitable sentencing of people of color, class and or poverty level as a whole is an example of abusing power, and is habitually problematic. The thousands of different ways that injustice can navigate through a system that's set up to stamp out the under privileged with little distinction is astonishing.

Because the judicial system constantly suffers from a full load of overworked public defenders, underpaid prosecutors and overwhelmed magistrates that take over the cases that officers present to them, it is imperative that the officer get the initial part of the arrest correct on the first attempt. That means, no surprises, no missing evidence, no skipped steps, no violation of rights, no overstepping authority, and no token of impropriety. Establish probable cause and enforce the law without prejudice or malice.

While naturally condemning criminality, the hands of "Lady Justice" remain contaminated. Ranging from atrocities such as false imprisonment and trumped up charges, to racial profiling and bigoted bias police work, these handicaps can reduce the competence and character that go into good policing, leading to a lifetime of regret and anguish, both personally and professionally.

Held to a higher standard in the current productive society, the title of being a police officer typically is accompanied by an irreproachable life style. This is why anyone serving in any kind of a law enforcement capacity is immediately viewed as being guilty until proven innocent whenever accused of wrong doing. Just the idea of impropriety can produce a disappointing and astonished outlook. This is also why most oaths taken by law enforcement officers involve a passage that reference living an unsullied life.

There are many scenarios that may transpire throughout an officer's career. Entirely based on actual events, End of the Thin Blue Line was created to introduce only a fraction of what a law enforcement officer may encounter at any given time during their tour. The events bravely shared in ETBL were used as a firsthand look and guide into the understanding of an officer's daily sacrifice.

End of the Thin Blue Line should be used as a tool to help navigate through any similar situations. Suicide, homicide, sexual assault, child abuse, social media abuse, consequential encounters, on and off duty encounters, comfort mistakes and calls to heroism are some of the topics that are featured throughout the journey within ETBL. Although ultimately, the decisions made in the field will solely belong to that agent of law enforcement, already in the field.

As a first responder, police officers are intimately exposed to the many dangers imbedded within the chaos that they chase. Physically, emotionally and psychologically, the charge of being a regulator for the safety of societal conflict can be daunting. With side effects that stretch from one end of the spectrum to the other, policing society can easily wage a war on one's psyche. From happiness and contentment, to anger and depression, officers are vulnerable. The hard truth of it is, most law enforcement officer's journey through their careers unaware of the next hazards that diabolically lay in wait just around the corner. Sometimes, officers are simply guilty of either not realizing the symptoms, or intentionally ignoring them all together; either out of shame, ignorance or arrogance. Exposed to triggers almost on a daily basis, this frame of mind can unwittingly change your childhood's dream career from a paradise, into a paradox.

Although proud of their service, dawning the badge can be a hard career to live with. It can have a residual effect on one's life. After what will seem like a life time of excitingly rewarding work, seemingly endless disappointments and heavy emotional moments, they will never be the same person as they started out as. With the clouded veil removed for a clearer, revealing view of the world, they will forever have the stain of mans' darkness imprinted in their minds. This is the burden that every officer will bear far beyond the end of their thin blue line tour.

Practicing the mediation of conscious balance, both socially and professionally should help during your career, but like any other type of investment, conscious balance can be monumental with helping to transition and or end careers. The habitual tendencies, reoccurring dreams and thought process developed over the years as a result of being an officer can become manageable, if they are acknowledged.

As a law enforcement officer your fundamental duty will be to enforce the law while reasonably safeguarding society. Ethical integrity, professional proficiency, training, experience, morality, patience and the ever-demanding sense of duty will become paramount in the process. A process similar to what the officers of ETBL diligently displayed.

Now that End of the Thin Blue Line helped you glance at a fraction of the demand of an officer, you're now positioned to ask yourself, can you do the same?

<u>Thank You</u>

First and foremost, I'd really like to thank all of the heroic individuals that trusted me with telling their story. Your sacrifices have already helped to save many. Now that a compilation of your life altering journeys can be used as an in-depth look into both, the scripted and unscripted duties of an officer, others can learn from those braved events which will continue to help guide and enlighten many more to come. From the average interested reader, to the reformed or misinformed individual, the rookie officer or the experienced officer, families of law enforcement, even the required reading for a college course, your contribution to ETBL will always be an index to understanding.

To all who wake up every day and pin the badge onto their chest, strap their gun belt to their waist, and go out to do what very few are willing to do, I salute you. Forever my brothers and sisters in blue, I would like to take this opportunity to thank you all. Especially everyone that I've ever had the personal pleasure of working with. You've always gotten me back home to my family, and I appreciate you for that every day.

To my family and friends that stuck around for the almost twenty year roller coaster, thank you too. Without your contributions and understanding, I probably would have submitted to any one of the multiple snares along the way.

To my precious daughter and son...there are no words to describe what you have unknowingly contributed to my life. To this day, I am truly blessed to have you in my corner...I love you both, and I thank you.

Most importantly, thank you Lord. Every day, I wake up with an abundance of testimonial faith. Knowing the things that I've experienced, witnessed or counseled first hand, I know that the fruits of my faith are confirmed through Him.

Finally, thank you to my readers. I pray that this glimpse into the anatomy of an officer helped you in understanding the daily demand and sacrifices that every officer faces.